LET'S BEGIN AGAIN

LET'S BEGIN AGAIN

by FATHER SHERWOOD

As told to Jamie Buckingham

LOGOS INTERNATIONAL / Plainfield, New Jersey

Scripture quotations are taken from the King James Version of the Bible.

Library of Congress Catalog Card Number: 74-33671
International Standard Book Number: 0-88270-117-7 (hardcover)
0-88270-118-5 (papercover)

Contents

Foreword

In his autobiographical novel, *Report to Greco*, Nikos Kazantzakis tells of an earnest young man who visited a saintly old monk on a remote island and asked him, "Do you still wrestle with the devil, father?"

The old man answered, "Not any longer, my child. I have grown old and he has grown old with me. He no longer has the strength . . . now I wrestle with God."

"With God!" exclaimed the young man wide-eyed. "Do you hope to win?"

"Oh, no, my son," came the answer. "I hope to lose."

Wrestling with God, it seems, has been a favorite pastime ever since that notorious match in the ring at Peniel close by the Brook Jabbok. To some, it's a sport. To others, it's a compulsion. To all, it is a futile effort. Even though the match goes on, God always wins.

I have learned something about the futility of such wrestling matches through my association with Father Sherwood. Spry, bouncy, and with a constant song coming from his lips, this octogenarian has made life joyful for all around him. His curly hair is snow-white and almost shoulder-length. Even though his full beard, the same color as his hair, hides his clerical collar, he still has the look and demeanor of an Old Testament prophet. Yet despite the fact he is twice my age, I have found my venerable confidant still wrestling with problems I thought were confined to those of my generation —sex, finances, family relations, rebellion against God.

On his first visit to our Florida home, I was taking Sherry through the house to his bedroom when my then nine-year-old daughter whispered to me from where she was hiding behind a door.

"Daddy, who's he?" she said fearfully.

"Moses!" I whispered reverently.

"Really!" she said, her eyes as big as two fried eggs.

Then Father Sherry confided he really wasn't Moses. Instead, he said, he was Jacob, still limping a bit from a recent bout of wrestling with God. It seems that Father Sherry's bouts intensified after he reached eighty, probably because he married a beautiful woman thirty years his junior.

I won't steal the good priest's delightful conclusion of this situation, nor will I divulge his trade secrets about how to get your get-up-and-go back after it got-up-and-went. That's what this book is all about—restoration and relationships.

Perhaps, to help make my point, it will be all right to borrow a few paragraphs from a recent letter, written by Father Sherry just after he passed his eighty-fourth birthday:

How wonderful our love life has become. Something happened just yesterday that points out the beauty of it all. During our recent trip to Florida, there was a good deal of frustration. Such things as being kept up late at night by well-meaning friends, and always, except during our stay at the Goldsmiths' in Melbourne, the old problem of single beds. I guess most folks think an eighty-four-year-old man would rather sleep alone than with his young bride.

As a result, Erma and I found our lovemaking pretty well limited to holding hands in the car. And it seemed the longer we were restrained from any serious love encounter, the easier it became to put it off. (Maybe this is one way my age *is* beginning to show itself.)

In any case, when I woke up early Wednesday, the morning after our return to Charlotte, I didn't have the longing for close physical contact with my still-sleeping wife that I had felt several times during the preceding eight days. I lay beside her warm body, praying, and remembering that I needed to prepare for a ten o'clock prayer meeting I was to conduct. I knew I should get out of bed and start studying. Yet, it was as if God Himself were telling me, "Make love to Erma."

I almost refused. I almost said No, arguing that I needed to get up, busy myself in my Bible, and let her sleep. After all, we had really been on each other's nerves the night before.

But the inner voice was quite clear. So I asked the Lord to do the impossible: to arouse me—and to have Erma ready when I reached for her.

The prayer was literally and beautifully answered. Neither of us spoke, yet with steadily mounting passion we came together in perfect consummation. As we exploded in our ecstasy, the room was suddenly filled with praise and music as our hearts overflowed through our voices. In prayer and song we praised God both in English and in our prayer language, recognizing the actual presence of the Father who was blessing our union.

Then came the "after passion," if I can call it that—the quieted but intense desire to melt into one another. It was sweeter and better than even the moments of strongest passion. Browning's words from *The Ring and the Book* come near to the perfect description:

> Because of our souls' yearning that we meet
> And mix in soul through flesh, which yours and mine
> Wear and impress and make their visible selves,

—All which means, for love of you and me
Let us become one flesh, being one soul.

I thank God for restoration of body and spirit. But far more exhilarating than any sensation of my youth is the sense of becoming "one soul" with my youthful bride.

But it has not always been such smooth sailing for this old priest. This is the story of how he wrestled with God—and how God has pinned him to the mat every time.

JAMIE BUCKINGHAM
Melbourne, Florida

Preface

Although neither Erma nor I hold degrees in psychology, we are frequently asked to serve as marriage counselors. I suspect this is because our consultants assume that if any two people as obviously mismated as Erma and I appear to be can be genuinely happy, then we must possess a secret formula which would enable any couple to secure the same results.

As a matter of fact, we do have such a secret, and it can be expressed in a workable formula: 1) keep the lines of communication open and speak the truth—no matter what the cost; 2) listen to what the other has to say; 3) let Jesus Christ become Lord of the problem areas of our lives—sex, finances, in-law relations, health, and creeping old age. Through these steps, we found God could turn a potentially disastrous marriage into one of beauty and happiness.

"But I'm not that religious," you might say.

Our reply is that we do not consider our secret of happiness to be religion. Rather it is life—a new kind of life. Religion did not save our faltering marriage, nor did it give my tired old body new potency. In fact, religion came nearer to wrecking our marriage than anything else. I tried to live a religious life and found it impossible. The demands to be holy drove me to a nervous breakdown and wrecked my body before I was forty years old. Gradually, I came to admit I was a failure—as a priest, as a husband, as a man.

"It is impossible to live the Christian life," I said one day in desperation. "Only Jesus could live such a life."

Then, at the age of seventy, I had an experience with the Holy Spirit—a life-changing, revolutionary experience which made Jesus real to me. And Jesus, living in my tired, ancient body, gave me new life.

That's not religion. That's reality.

Erma and I had everything going against us. From our wedding night, when she discovered I was not a gallant prince, but a wrinkled, impotent old man—through the fears of growing old without money—through the horrible quarrels over each other's children—the marriage seemed doomed to failure.

Yet we two incompatible persons, rather than seek divorce, decided to stick it out and seek God's best solution. For us, it was find God's plan—or perish. And in those early days, we came much nearer perishing than we like to recall.

Fortunately, in the midst of our incompatibility, my wife and I had one thing in common: we both wanted to please God. And Erma was determined to make this marriage work by telling me the truth about myself whenever the opportunity arose—often in vivid phraseology. These infusions of truth did more for me than potency pills and advice from friends ever did. Painfully, yet gloriously, we discovered that when Jesus Christ becomes Lord, life begins again—even at eighty.

Therefore, taking a line from the young people who swarm through our lives, we have decided to tell it like it is. While this book will be embarrassing to some, we believe it will be immensely helpful to many more. You see, we know that the first whispered question our friends asked of each other when Erma and I announced our marriage was, "Is it possible for that eighty-year-old man to sexually satisfy that young woman?" And we're not ashamed to answer that unasked question by saying, "Without Jesus, no. But hallelujah, with Jesus, yes!"

I realize that because Erma and I talk about our sex life with simple, Christian naturalness, some will think I am obsessed by the subject and in some diluted way am really a "dirty old man" at heart. We are willing to run the risk of that accusation because we believe that the same formula which gave Abraham potency when he was a hundred and twenty years old is available today. Indeed, I have discovered it.

I mention sex in this preface—at the risk of being labeled a dirty old man—not because it looms as the only basis of a happy marriage, but because it is important. We have abundant proof that the people of God are often the very ones who need to rethink their whole attitude toward the subject. Many quiet tragedies lie hidden behind the outward smiles of valiant saints whose marital relations are a shambles. In contrast to the outspokenness of the modern generation, there is almost a conspiracy of silence among the people of God when it comes to sex. Thus, if no one else will speak up, then let it go on record that there is one eighty-five-year-old man who is willing to testify that not only did God create sex, He made it extremely pleasurable.

In the book, we also deal with God's plan for victory over

financial problems, the fear of old age, even submission to the church. However, since we do talk frankly about our sex experiences, we are resigned to the fact that some folks will remember no more. And perhaps that is the way it should be, for if the people of God can be helped in this area, then there is hope in the other areas as well.

So Erma and I invite you into our lives. Our masks are off that you may see how God can restore strength and joy to broken lives and withered bodies.

The secret (which we reveal ahead of time) is found in the formula: *Luvaluia!* That's it. Love one another *and* praise the Lord!

1
Let's Begin Again!

Side by side we lay in that narrow twin bed in John's room, my bride of four weeks and I. The blankets were pulled up over our nearly naked bodies, for the borrowed room was cold in the November dawn. An hour earlier we had both wakened and Erma's whispered love had drawn me from my bed on the other side of this little room to hold her in a tight embrace. Our passion had been real, if a bit frightening, to my eighty-year-old body. But now, as usual, had come once more the moment of truth. I simply was unable to perform as a man. The anguish of disappointment, the fear of impotency. It was all so real.

Our passion slowly ebbed, as the tide recedes on the beach, leaving behind the moss-covered rocks. We lay quietly, our bodies close, our spirits miles apart. I was trying very hard to keep from touching her soft, yielding flesh. We had quarreled, which had become our pattern when I was unable to satisfy her, and each of us had said things we wished had been left unspoken. Now, in the silence, she seemed so relaxed. I felt sure, however, that inside she was like me—a seething caldron of emotions. How right, I thought, my sister had been.

I could still hear the tones of Leila's voice. We had stopped at her home in Alexandria, Virginia—Erma, my daughter Margie, and I—only six weeks ago. I had been so proud and eager to show off Erma who only two days before had consented to be my fiancée. I was sure Leila and her husband, the General, would love her and shower me with congratulations. But Leila had taken me aside rather sternly.

"Bill," she said, "I cannot feel that it is right for you to marry a woman so much younger than yourself. She seems a fine person, and so are you. But you are eighty years old, and Erma is only fifty—two years younger than your daughter. It is not being fair to her. She has a right to expect more out of marriage than you are able to give her."

There was enough truth in what she was saying to give me momentary qualms. But I stoutly defended my plans. "Sis, I know I can make her happy, and that is all that really counts." I had meant it, too. But oh, how right Leila had been all the time. I had not been fair to Erma, and probably not to my daughter nor to myself.

I had assured Leila I would take my time, as she suggested. Yet less than two weeks later, Erma and I were on our way to Mexico on a surprise honeymoon trip.

True, we had not had a real wedding from a legal point of view. Yet did the blessing of Caesar—a license to marry from the state of North Carolina—make that much difference? Perhaps it did. Perhaps this whole affair was wrong.

Then came the disappointment. What I so vividly dreamed about disappeared in the swirling mist of fantasy. I was, as Leila had predicted, a dried-up old man. Was our failure to conform with human conventions the underlying reason why I had gone to sleep so many nights and wakened so many early mornings to find myself impotent? Passionate, yes. Able to arouse my wife. But always thwarted because of my lack of virile youth. What other word was there beside this one I hated so—*impotent!* Oh God, what can I do?

The early light of the November dawn was beginning to filter through the parted drapes in our Charlotte bedroom. I was really trying to pray now, but the prayer bounced off the ceiling. I was simply not getting through to God. I thought of how hurt Erma had looked when once, on our honeymoon, I had excused my lack of virility by saying that maybe it was God's judgment on our having "jumped the gun," by trying to enjoy married love there in Mexico before we had been married in accordance with the laws of the land. So hurt was she, so frightened really, that I had backed down and temporized. This had made matters all the worse, for she saw through me with her usual devastating clarity.

"Sherry, don't you know what you really believe?" she had asked me. "You told me that if God approved of it, it was all right for us to be married as we were. All we needed was a witness to represent society and a minister to represent Christ's church. And we had both. You said that a marriage license was just a man-made custom. Now you are saying that God may not have approved of it. Don't you know?"

I twisted and groaned inwardly. I did *not* know what I believed. I, an Episcopal priest for all these years, who had given counsel to so many others, why had I failed so badly in my own case?

More than once, I had heard Erma laughingly say, "It's not everyone who gets a husband, father, and priest all in one package." Yet I had failed her as a husband, and now came the crushing realization that I had also failed her as a priest.

Was I to be relegated to the role of a father—or a grandfather—instead of enjoying the tenderness of married love?

Yet stubborn pride would not let me do the one thing I longed to do, needed to do—reach out and touch her as a token of real love and forgiveness.

"Oh God, will You forgive me," I murmured to myself. But my prayer died aborning, for prayer that does not move a man to action is not true prayer, only words of self-pity. I needed to touch Erma, to apologize for the words spoken in the heat of the quarrel. Yet I continued as I was, proud, unrelenting, blocking my relationship with God as well as with my bride.

Erma, I had discovered, really had no bedroom of her own in this little house where she lived in Charlotte. It had been her home for twenty-three years, first with Jack White as his wife, and then for nine years as a widow with her four children. Now, at the age of eighty, I had taken on the responsibility of this ready-made family which included besides a love-starved wife, three teenagers and a twenty-two-year-old.

David was fourteen, a husky, well-developed boy, a member of the football team at Sedgefield Junior High. He was the only one of the four who called me "Pop." Nancy, seventeen, was brown-eyed, petite (though inclined to be plump like her mother), and almost ready to graduate at Myers Park High School. Also like her mother, she called me plain "Sherry." Robert, nineteen, was a junior at UNCC and commuted daily by car pool. He was a tall, hard-working, deeply reserved boy whom I wanted to get to know better. To him, I was "Father Sherwood." I was gratified to learn he had told his mother, "It will really be neat to have a minister in the family."

Then there was John, now twenty-two, whose bedroom we used whenever he was away for the night. Otherwise, I usually spent the night at my apartment on the other side of town which I had shared with my daughter. Occasionally we used Nancy's room, the one room with a double bed, while Nancy slept on the living room sofa. The house was too small for five adults, with its one bathroom and only one real bedroom. And now we were six. How had I ever thought that I could just move right in among them? But such practical difficulties are relegated to the back of your mind when you are in love and longing to be married.

This matter of where we would live was simply one of the problems I had ignored. Now I wondered. Had my haste to marry and "get on with our ministry" actually been a cruel trick of the devil? Deane Ballard must have thought it all right, or he would not have given way to our desire to be married even before we had our license. Why did I always have to be in such a hurry? Were our problems part of God's punishment because we had acted in haste and in disobedience to the civil laws?

How different it had all been in the weeks just before our marriage. How utterly, incredibly different! There had been those delicious after-midnight conversations on the telephone, when neither of us could bear to hang up and go back to sleep. The hour did not matter; our love made us tireless. There had been those long, long silences, our spirits actually touching. "We're just like two teenagers!" I could still hear Erma's chuckle. I loved her laughter. Then another silence, just a throbbing sense of love coming over the miles of copper wire. And with it, an ever mounting desire creeping over my old body, wiping out the years. I was in my twenties again, "young and lusty as an eagle," as the Psalmist put it. And while I recognized the sensation as erotic, there was something so pure and beautiful and tender about it all that I felt spiritually right in yielding to it.

Sadly, however, it just never occurred to me, in the budding sense of virility that now gripped me, that while my libido might be as strong as that of a young man, my ability to satisfy the normal desires of a healthy young woman might not have kept pace with that desire. The words "impotent old man" which I was now hearing bitterly from a gloating devil, had never entered my mind. Wasn't I strong, vigorous, and muscular? Indeed, I had begun anew ten years before at that C.F.O. camp in Ardmore, Oklahoma, when I had been baptized in the Holy Spirit. Lately, I had been jogging two miles a day, I could chin myself like a youngster (and boast of it, too), yet when it came to performance in bed—I was a failure.

Before we had gotten married, David had said to his mother, "Mom, I thought I would have a strong tall father, not an old man who looks like Moses."

I had danced up and down when Erma told me, "Honey, we'll just show them that age doesn't make a bit of difference when a person has been baptized in the Holy Spirit." What a braggadocian statement that had been. Confidently, I had shown David pictures of me on that football team of sixty years before, thinking that would convince him of my prowess. Instead, he had snickered—and I had blown up.

"Face up, Sherry, sex is for the young. Already, after only four weeks of marriage, you're dreading the nights. You're a failure." How sharp were the barbs of Satan.

"Oh God, help me out of this mess! Oh God, You can do what I cannot do. Help me, for Erma's sake. It's not her fault, Lord . . ."

The prayer was real this time. So real it was out loud. But I stopped as I heard a stifled sound coming from the pillow where Erma's blond head was half-buried. Was it a sob? No, even worse, she was laughing. It's bad enough to be criticized, even condemned, for being impotent. But to be laughed at is the worst of all insults.

I started to shrivel, but instead I thought, "Well, praise the Lord, at least she's seeing the humor rather than the tragedy."

"What's funny?" I asked meekly.

She turned over, wide awake, her eyes sparkling. "Do you remember what Lucille said the day before we were married in her house?"

The thrill was back. With the soft touch of her hand on my body, I suddenly felt closer to God. The ugly resentment against my own self, which included this dear victim of my haste and folly, had dropped away, and things were right side up once more.

"Don't you remember? Lucille said, 'Erma, I love you like a daughter, and I'm telling you, you can't marry that old man. You can eat three meals a day with him, but you just cannot go to bed with him!' " Her laughter twinkled.

"If she only knew," Erma giggled. "Going to bed with you isn't the worst of it. It's eating those three meals a day with you. Honey, where did you get those table manners? You know, I sometimes think you eat just like an animal."

Not only was I impotent, I was a caveman at the dinner table. I used my fingers like a fork and spoon and slurped my food with all the grace of a pig at the trough. I winced, yet at the same time I thanked God. We were over the hump, communicating happily once again. I had been so clumsy, and my resentment had not made matters better even if it had been directed mostly against my own self. Praise God, she had no resentment at all. Her words were really those of a mother scolding a loved child, not those of a frustrated, unfulfilled wife. I breathed a prayer of very real gratitude.

"We'll get there yet," I whispered, holding her hand tightly. "Isn't it wonderful the way God lets us begin again?"

"Oh, yes," she murmured, turning toward me, her lips brushing against the side of my face. "We'll begin all over again, with Jesus." Her soft hand caressed me gently, and I pressed her more closely to me. For a few minutes we lay in that relaxed sweetness. Desire, eros, had gone, but peace had replaced the turmoil. God's own peace held us close together. It was almost as I had imagined it might be, as if our married love had been fulfilled in perfect consummation. We started to pray, our morning prayer of thanksgiving which we had determined would always be the first thing in our lives, but which up to this morning had been forgotten. I held her still more closely after the time of prayer. We kissed, my lips drinking in the sweetness of her. I felt desire swelling back. Now, I thought happily, now is the moment.

But suddenly the alarm went off in the boys' room and we heard them beginning to stir. This was a school day, and we sprang apart, for the door was ajar in the bedroom.

"No privacy at all," Erma sighed. "The story of my life—"

She was interrupted by David's shrill voice. "Mom, where's my socks? Mom, where's my—" And mom was up, hunting for mislaid socks and shirts. Even so, I was singing a little song of praise down deep inside. Erma still loved me, and what was almost better, I knew that I really loved her. And God would work out the rest if we'd just give Him time.

On that note, I stretched once or twice and sat up on the edge of John's bed, hunting for my own socks. How things did manage to get lost in this house. Never mind. We would begin again.

2

"Luvaluia"

When you come right down to it, why had Erma and I gotten married? The question haunted my mind.

Erma had driven me across town to the apartment which I had shared with my daughter, Margie, during the nine months I had lived in Charlotte. I needed to write some letters, pay some bills, and make a few phone calls. Such things were impossible to do at Erma's helter-skelter house. Now, most of my tasks accomplished, I leaned back in my chair beside the battered old desk, determined to think things through.

We had meant it when we had said to one another a few hours before that with God's help we would begin again. But some of the things Erma had blurted out during that early morning hour of frustration and quarreling still rankled.

I rummaged in my desk drawer for my quiet-time book, my spiritual diary. I had kept books of notes like this off and on for many years. Glancing through the pages which had been written in the weeks just before our marriage, my eyes caught the words, ". . . all your life up to the present moment has been a preparation for what is still ahead." The words came from a time when God had spoken to me. It was part of "the prophecies," as I had called them, a part of what I believed to be messages to me from the Lord. As things were working out, I wondered if they had been really from the Lord after all.

I knew, of course, that God can and does speak to His people today. I had known that as a matter of experience, not just theory, ever since my re-conversion to Christ forty years before, in my association with the Oxford Group, started by Sam Shoemaker. Through many long years, I had formed the habit of writing down thoughts that I felt were inspired by the Holy Spirit. On many occasions, I had known real blessings as I carried out directives given me in the times of quiet meditation when I sat with Bible and notebook in hand. But these particular notes had come to me in a different way; and somehow, when I wrote them down, they seemed to possess greater authenticity than my usual quiet-time notes. These thoughts had seemed not so much mine as given me from without. Just writing them down had given me a sense of exultation hard to describe.

I read a little further in my "q.t.b.," skipped a bit here and there, read two or three pages at random. There was such a note of quiet assurance in it all! It seemed that God had a special task for me to perform, and somehow Erma White was deeply involved in it. Marriage to her had come into the picture, at first as a possibility half glimpsed, then as something which God Himself had ordained for us. But was this really a message from the Lord—or just the wishful thinking of an old man of eighty, twice widowed, falling in love with an attractive widow two years younger than his daughter? If these messages were really prophecies from the

Lord, why was the present reality so painfully different from
what the messages had led me to expect? I slipped the
notebook back into my desk drawer and settled back in my
easy chair once more, resolved to think it all through.

Erma's father had been the village blacksmith in the little
hamlet of West Paris, Maine. We were both transplanted
northerners, for I hailed from Rochester, New York. Erma's
first husband, Jack White, had also been a New Yorker. An
engineer, he had brought his bride to Charlotte twenty-three
years ago. Death had claimed him, still too young, nine years
ago.

On the other hand, I had been a widower for only four
years, and if there was anything settled in my thinking, it was
that I would certainly not marry for a third time. For one
thing, my daughter, Margie, who had come to make her
home with me at the death of her stepmother, needed my
care and attention. She suffered from arthritis. Although able
to be up and around, she was unable to hold a full-time job.
Besides this, I valued my complete freedom to "exercise my
ministry"—whatever that was. As a retired priest of the
Episcopal church, now endowed with new energy and health
through my experience with the Baptism in the Holy Spirit, I
felt called back into some kind of active service, even though
I was no longer qualified to hold a parish of my own. I did
manage to keep busy, traveling by bus to the various parts of
the country, frequently accompanied by Margie, giving talks
before groups of charismatic Christians. Frankly, I felt I had
lived a full life, and I was ready to slow down, speaking a
little here and there, and gradually sinking into a rocking
chair as I had been told that all octogenarians ought to do.

After the death of my second wife in 1965, Margie and I made our home in Mexico. It had been an enjoyable, happy, three years as I served as volunteer righthand man to the Bishop of Guadalajara, the Right Reverend Melchor Saucedo. Returning to the States, we settled in Charlotte, partially on the encouragement of Mary Marshall Young (Mrs. Dolph Young) who had written me saying a women's prayer group in which I had once ministered would be delighted if I made the Queen City my home. They even offered to assist us in finding an apartment.

"It will be great to have a minister as our leader and teacher," Mary Marshall wrote. "We hope that, as a retired Episcopal priest, you will have plenty of time to devote to us."

Within a week after moving to Charlotte, we met Deane Ballard. This young Presbyterian minister was an exceptional Bible teacher, and we easily found our place at his Wednesday morning meeting in Lucille Buening's home. This, combined with a Monday morning meeting in the beautiful home of Tom and Charlotte Hawthorne, plus an occasional speaking engagement kept me busy.

It was in these groups that I met Erma. I knew her first as a shy, retiring widow who seldom opened her mouth at the meetings. Later, she called my apartment, offering to take me shopping to pick up a few needed items for the kitchen. It was a delightful expedition, properly chaperoned by Erma's friend, Kay Burwell. During the course of the afternoon, I found that the silent, smiling widow of the prayer group could also be a chatty, laughing companion—the kind I realized I had been without for so long.

A week later, I found myself sitting beside her at the Bible class in the Buening home. I thanked her for the help she and Kay had given me the week before. Erma brushed aside my thanks with a smile. "Luvaluia," she said.

"What's 'luvaluia'?" I asked.

"I don't know," she shrugged, laughing. "It's just a word that came to me two years ago when someone prayed for me."

I could hardly wait until the class was over to share my interpretation of her word. "Love is what the world is starving for," I told her excitedly as I cornered her in the den. " 'Hallelujah' is a Hebrew word which means 'Praise the Lord.' What a perfect combination! Love people—like God loves them—and keep praising the Lord as you do it."

The next week Erma drew me aside in the hallway. "Father Sherwood, would you and Margie have supper with my son John and me some night soon? I want you to get to know him so you'll know better how to pray for him. I guess you've heard me asking the prayer group to pray. The doctors say he has leukemia, but we are trusting God to heal him."

We lingered in the doorway, talking, and she began to share about John. "It was Good Friday when he called me from the Naval Hospital in Portsmouth," she said. "He was studying to become a doctor when he got out of the Navy and was checking his own blood in the lab when he found leukemia cells."

"I'd like very much to know him," I said. "Can we make it this Friday night?"

I loved John White from the start. He had been at death's door, but now, thanks to much prayer and careful medication, the disease was in a state of remission. In fact, John was even up and skiing. We had dinner at one of Charlotte's finest restaurants, and over flickering candlelight, John and I planned a trip over to Canton in the western part of the state to hear the Reverend Dennis Bennett speak in an Episcopal church. I had known Dennis for some time. An Episcopal priest from Seattle, he was one of the prime movers in the charismatic movement which was sweeping the nation. Perhaps, I thought, Dennis and his lovely wife, Rita, would pray for John's healing.

We made our trip, and John was impressed with the way Dennis and Rita presented the healing mission of the Church, feeling it less emotional than some of the presentations he had seen. A few days later, he volunteered to go with Margie and me to hear the Bennetts again, this time at a Regional Convention of the Full Gospel Business Men's Fellowship International in Greensboro. This time Erma also attended these meetings, and drove home with John and me while Margie went back in another car. I had given up my driver's license while living in Mexico, but between Erma and John, I now had a chauffeur for my trips to the various prayer groups where I was invited to share.

Summer came, and for my daughter and me, there was the joy of a trip to Ireland and England with a group of Spirit-baptized Christians. It was a glorious two weeks for all of us. We had close fellowship with portions of "the Body," as we called those deeply committed groups with no particular denominational affiliation. From Ireland, we moved on down to South Chard, England, a tiny village in Devonshire, to spend ten days in the homes of happy, deeply devoted members of the Body there. It was here I met Harry Greenwood who, along with the South Chard group, would play a big part in Erma's and my future.

In the fall of that year, after I had resumed my routine in Charlotte, Erma called me one day to make an appointment for special counseling. After she arrived at my apartment, I excitedly asked if she would be willing to listen to a tape recording of one of the lively services in South Chard. Of course, she had no choice but to agree, so I started the tape and sat back, enjoying once again the singing and worship of that wonderful group in Devonshire. I could almost picture Uncle Sid Purse, standing in the corner, dancing stiff-legged as the others sang the lively Scripture choruses.

Suddenly I realized the tape was over, and I had been asleep. I was mortified. How long? I wondered. How like an old man to invite in a beautiful woman and then go to sleep in her presence. I was chagrined, but Erma brushed my apologies aside with a laugh. "I really didn't know what I was going to say to you anyway," she giggled. "I'm grateful God let you go to sleep. Maybe we can counsel some other time."

Then, just as she was leaving my study, she turned back. "Father Sherry, there is one thing I do wish you would pray about. Please ask God to find me a good second husband."

"Fine," I said. But even as I said it, I felt my throat going dry. "What are the specifications?" I asked.

"Just that he be a real Christian," Erma smiled. "With a good sense of humor. He'll need it." She left then, leaving behind the echo of her tinkling laughter. But the room seemed strangely empty as I heard the outer door close behind her.

3

Exorcism—and Holy Laughter

It was ten o'clock Monday morning, and the prayer group women were assembling in Charlotte Hawthorne's spacious home. A little knot stood drinking their coffee in the dining room to the left of the entrance foyer. A few others had seated themselves in the big living room on the other side. Late arrivals were still coming in the open front door. Serious work lay ahead. There were so many needs to pray about.

Foremost in everyone's mind was Mary Lynn Stockdale. Martha Kale, who had not yet arrived at the meeting, had told us about Mary Lynn. A month before, this young mother of three small children had been rushed to the Presbyterian Hospital just in time to save her life from a heavy overdose of barbiturates. We knew Mary Lynn was still in need of much prayer, although she was now home from the hospital.

The phone rang and Charlotte called Erma to take it. Moments later, Erma was back. "It's Martha," Erma said.

"Mary Lynn's desperate—out of her head. She needs help now."

"You'll have to get out there yourself," someone said. "Take Father Sherry. Go on, hurry. We'll keep praying for you here."

I bundled into the car beside Erma. The Stockdales lived outside the city limits. Fortunately, traffic was light at this hour, and we made good time. We arrived to find a police car pulling away from the house. Noticing my clerical collar, they called out to us. "Some dame was threatening suicide," the young officer said. "Our siren must have scared her from doing anything, but she sure needs help."

Three youngsters, all under five and wide-eyed with fright, huddled in the doorway. We could hear moaning sounds, punctuated by hysterical screams, coming down the stairwell. Bounding up the stairs, we encountered Martha.

"Can I ever use some help," she groaned. "She's out of her head."

We told Martha to take care of the children while we took over with Mary Lynn.

Mary Lynn Stockdale was a beautiful young woman in her late twenties. But that morning, she was anything but beautiful. Fully clothed, she lay twisting and thrashing on the bed. "Let me die!" she wailed. "Oh, please let me die!"

She was half sobbing, half screaming the words as she writhed back and forth like a snake. I had never before seen anyone in such an extreme depression. Clearly, it was demonic torture. I had enough experience as a priest to know what I must do in a situation like this.

"You pray, Erma," I told my companion, "and I'll cast the spirits out."

Wordlessly, Erma dropped on her knees beside the

prostrate, writhing girl, while I stood at the foot of the bed and invoked the aid of the Almighty. I knew that I must do exactly what Jesus, on numerous occasions, had told His followers to do. I must not ask Him to cast out the demons that were tormenting this young mother; I must do it myself—in His name.

"Lord, in Your mighty name I take dominion!" I began. "Cover us all, cover this whole house, and everyone in it, with Your precious blood. Let the blood be our protection against the whole power of the enemy!" With a strong prayer of affirmation, I bound Satan against further hurting this poor girl, who was obviously being tortured and tormented by the powers of hell.

But the screaming and writhing, the snakelike tortured twisting, continued even as I commanded the tormenting spirits to loose her. For perhaps ten minutes I persisted. Erma remained quietly on her knees beside the bed, her face like that of an angel as she prayed under her breath. Mary Lynn seemed as far from quieting down as ever. Why was not my prayer getting through to God?

"Oh Lord God," I prayed, "I feel so helpless. Give me discernment. Give me a word of wisdom. Tell me what to say." Almost instantly, the words were on my lips. I stopped talking to the demons, and spoke loudly, authoritatively, to the young woman herself.

"Mary Lynn, listen to me. Listen hard. This is life or death! There is someone who has wronged you greatly, and you have never forgiven him. I don't know who this person is, but you do. That's true, isn't it?"

She stopped her twisting and nodded violently.

"All right, then, Mary Lynn, forgive him! Forgive him. And do it now. Quickly. There is no time to lose."

The screams and writhing had stopped now. Groggily, Mary Lynn rose to a sitting position on the edge of the bed. She rubbed her eyes and wiped her face. Although she was breathing hard, she was finally in command of herself. The struggle, however, going on deep inside was mirrored in her face.

She spoke for the first time, in a soft husky voice. "Yes, father, there is someone." Then she pressed her hands more tightly over her face and held them there. "But oh, father—I can't forgive him. I just don't feel forgiving toward him." The wailing, the hysteria, seemed to be about to begin all over again.

"Mary Lynn, you must say it. Say, 'God, I forgive him as You have forgiven me.' "

"But I tell you I can't! I can't! He ruined my life! Oh, let me die!"

"Mary Lynn!" I spoke sternly. At that moment, I knew that I had all the authority of Christ Himself. Those demons torturing this lovely young woman were the enemies of God. They *must* come out. "Mary Lynn!" I said again. "I couldn't care less how you *feel*. I do care, God cares, what you *do*. You must say those words."

Mary Lynn's Roman Catholic training came through, as she recognized the authority of a priest. Her defenses shattered, she said meekly, "Okay, father, I'll say it. God, I forgive him."

The miracle took place before our eyes. Even as she spoke the words, life seemed to return to her face. She collapsed on the bed with her face in the pillow, but her sobbing indicated life rather than death. "Oh God, oh God . . ." she wept over and over again. But this time no longer in desperation. Now it was in profound release. The worst of the struggle was over. At the name of the Lord Jesus Christ, the demons had to flee, once she was obedient to forgive.

Erma, I suddenly realized, had flinched even more than Mary Lynn at the sternness of my voice as I spoke to the demons. But she was ready now to play her part. Softly she began to croon, oh so softly, one after another of the little chorus songs we were so accustomed to singing in the prayer-group meetings. She seemed to know them all. Ten or fifteen minutes passed as I stood, transfixed, watching the little scene. Then I shook myself loose, turned toward the stairway, and beckoned Erma to come with me. Surely Mary Lynn was fast asleep by now. But Erma only smiled and shook her head slightly, her fingers to her mouth in a gesture I understood.

"You go on down," she whispered. "Martha has to go and will need your help with the children." I nodded, and Erma resumed the soft crooning to the now sleeping girl beside whom she knelt.

Minutes later, Erma tiptoed down to join the children and me. Martha had gone, and we finished giving the children their meal. All the while, a thought was running through my head: How heavenly it would be to go on ministering to God's children with this same, sweet, gentle woman as my companion. But I knew I must not indulge this thought. I had firmly decided never to marry again, to devote the closing years of a long life to taking care of my daughter. Obviously, a third marriage was not for me.

But try as I would, I could not escape the train of thought this visit to Mary Lynn's had quickened in me. Would marriage be possible for me, a man of eighty? Not just *a* marriage, but *real* marriage, marriage to a woman like Erma? I was unable to squelch the thought. Something that would not be denied had awakened in me, and I liked the way it felt. Could it be that God would grant me, in the twilight years of my life, the relationship I had so yearned for with my second wife, Thelma, but which, had eluded my grasp? Could it happen with Erma?

Perhaps that is why, when something happened a week later, I recognized it as a great turning point in both of our lives. It began when I learned that my friend Archer Torrey of Korea was in town. I had first met Archer, the grandson of one of the world's great Bible teachers, R. A. Torrey, about six years ago in St. Petersburg. A fellow Episcopal priest, he had looked me up on his furlough when he learned that I, too, had experienced the Baptism in the Holy Spirit, which at that time was still unusual among Episcopal clergymen.

Born in China of Presbyterian missionary parents, Archer had become an Episcopalian, gone out to Korea as a missionary, and there had established Jesus Abbey, a unique contribution to the missionary field. Jesus Abbey is a place of prayer and praise for Christian and non-Christian alike, a place where Koreans can learn practical farming and other skills to enable them to make the most of their country's limited natural resources. Jesus Abbey was only a dream when I'd first met this fine young priest. Now it had become a solid, successful reality—a model for many similar projects. Since Archer's lovely wife, Jane, was from Charlotte, and Jane and Erma were good friends, it was natural they would head this way on their furlough.

I called Archer and invited him to our apartment for lunch. Margie was away in the north for a visit, but that did not matter. I asked some of the prayer-group folks in to enjoy sukiyaki. Of course Erma White was invited to help.

By all reckoning, the party was a success. The sukiyaki

made a real hit, and the fellowship between those Spirit-filled Christians ran high. Archer had me worried a little, though. He looked thin and tired. It had been a hard winter for him, he confided, and he felt the strain.

The dishes cleared away, the group relaxed in the living room. I had trouble keeping my eyes off Erma, who always seemed to be in my line of sight. Suddenly I heard myself saying—and to this minute I cannot say what prompted me, unless it was the Holy Spirit—"I think Erma would like to have us pray for her to receive the Baptism in the Holy Spirit."

Erma smiled quietly and said simply, "You do?" But she did not hold back. She sat relaxed in a chair we pulled out to the center of the room and waited peacefully while Archer and I prayed in turn. Then both of us laid hands on her head and asked the Lord to fill her to overflowing with His Holy Spirit. Most times when I prayed for people like this, they began immediately to speak in tongues—just as the early disciples of Jesus did at Pentecost. But with Erma, I learned God does not always do things in the usual ways.

Instead of the expected flow of strange syllables, there suddenly poured from Erma's mouth a peal of joyous laughter. It was heavenly laughter, peal after peal, a burst of the happiest, most infectious laughter I had ever heard. So contagious was it that I began laughing myself without knowing why. So did Archer. Soon everyone in the room was laughing. We sat down in chairs to keep from rolling on the floor. It was pure mirth as we yielded to the joyous infection. We were not laughing because there was anything funny— but because our happiness was so great that only laughter could express it.

When at last we calmed down enough to talk rationally,

Erma looked at me. "Father Sherry, are you disappointed that I didn't speak in tongues?"

What could I say? Who can box in the Holy Spirit? Even if Erma never spoke in tongues, her manifestation of heavenly laughter was far more evidence of the move of the Holy Spirit in her life than most folks ever received. As it had been for me ten years ago, so it was now with Erma. The beginning of a new life in the Spirit.

4

Love Blooms

The October sun was just peeking through the eastern trees when Erma made her first stop for gas. We were on our way to those eagerly anticipated meetings of the Holy Spirit Teaching Mission (now called Christian Growth Ministries) in Hollywood, Florida. There was no doubt of it, Erma's Chrysler Imperial was a definite improvement over the Greyhound bus. Well before nightfall, we should be at the house of Judge and Ruth Jernigan on St. Simon's Island, Georgia. I would speak at the regular Friday night prayer group in their home, and then stay on to preach in their Episcopal church in the absence of the rector.

Sprawled out comfortably on the back seat of the big car, I gave myself over to dozing and daydreaming while Erma and Margie conversed in low tones in front. Things had moved rapidly these last ten days. A call on a sick man the night before had kept me up late, and our predawn start had seemed terribly early. Then, not until after we were underway did Erma confess she had never driven more than a hundred miles on any trip. However, I expected things to improve as we moved down the road.

Mile after mile we sped along the South Carolina highway, stopping at noon for lunch, then down across the tip of Georgia to Brunswick and out the bridges to St. Simon's Island. Shortly afterward, we were resting under the stately live oaks in the Jernigans' front yard. Also there to greet us was an eighty-year-old woman, Christy, who now lived permanently with the judge and his wife. A retired nurse, Christy had been a great teacher of the Bible in her day, but she was now so deaf it was next to impossible to communicate with her. Only Ruth seemed to be able to make her understand.

Ruth and Judge Jernigan had prepared a full schedule for us—an informal meeting that first night, and larger gatherings the next two, besides some daytime informal teaching sessions. I reveled in it. These earnest seekers were the kind who draw one out, who call out the very best in a teacher. I was grateful to see how well Erma, Margie, and Ruth got along together, even though they had not met before. It was "the fellowship of the Holy Ghost," the closest of all fraternities.

Saturday afternoon, Erma and I shared a time of counseling with Ruth Jernigan. Life had posed some hard problems for Ruth, and she welcomed this opportunity to open up to us. Once again, as at Mary Lynn's home, I felt a very strong bond of spiritual understanding between Erma and myself as we ministered together. None of this escaped Christy, who although deaf of ear, was discerning of eye. She pulled Erma aside and said, "I have an idea that Sherry likes you." Being deaf, she said it so loud that the entire neighborhood could hear. However, instead of being embarrassed, I was pleased. I did like Erma, a great deal.

Sunday, I accompanied the judge to a little Episcopal church on the mainland where I preached. Later, I held communion service and preached at the church on the island of which the Jernigans were communicants. I grasped the chance to preach to these good people about salvation—a subject so often ignored in the established, denominational churches. As always, when this simple message is proclaimed, it went to the hearts of the people. Many met me at the door to thank me, some with tears in their eyes. Their expressions of gratitude were so different from the perfunctory "Good sermon, Rector," which used to be my portion as I shook hands with the flock at the doors of the churches I had served. How far behind me that seemed now.

That afternoon, upon the request of the Jernigans and Christy, a crowd of us gathered at their swimming pool and sang joyfully as I officiated at the water baptism of Christy, the judge, and his lady. What a perfect symbol, I thought, this plunging under the water and rising up again. I was glad our Episcopal prayer book had provision for baptism by immersion, though it is seldom used. Erma whispered to me that she was much tempted to join the three in being immersed. "But I'm not quite ready," she confessed. "Perhaps there will be another chance before too long."

It was late Wednesday evening, after the second full day of the conferences in Hollywood, Florida, before we had a chance to talk much again. Erma, Margie, and I sat relaxed in the living room of the little house loaned us by my old friend, Ed Raits. Margie was talking about times past,

recalling those dark, arid years of my life after I had a
nervous breakdown and virtually left the church to go into
the radio business. She recalled I had been so bitter and
confused that I had almost refused to go to church when she
had been confirmed—after all those earlier years as a priest.

I winced at the telling. It was not pleasant to recall those
years when I'd literally bowed God out of my life. My
daughter had been in her teens at the time, my older son,
Bill, was just entering adolescence and Bob, my younger son,
had just been born. I had simply run away from God and the
exercise of my priesthood. True, I had come back to God
with all my heart, and in a way, for the first time, I really
knew Him as Lord. Yet how deep were the scars inflicted
upon my children because their daddy turned his heart away
from God.

Erma, though, was only half listening. She was caught up
in the spirit of the conference meetings—especially the
messages of Harry Greenwood, that same joyful man I had
met in England. But something was sour inside me. The
more Erma talked about Harry Greenwood, the more upset I
got. I knew Harry was attractive and had great faith, but why
didn't Erma see that I was a much more suitable teacher
than he? After all, I knew her real needs, and she had met
Harry only the day before.

The next night, it was the same thing. Margie had gone to
bed early since she was exhausted, but Erma wanted to sit up
and talk about Harry Greenwood. "He was better than ever,"
she sighed. "Oh, for a faith like that."

I muttered something about liking the messages of Derek
Prince, one of the other speakers at the conference. Erma
must not have heard me, for she bubbled on.

"I have an appointment with Harry for tomorrow," she

said. "Will you say a prayer for me before we turn in, that I'll
find what I'm looking for?"

I prayed, but my heart wasn't in it. Why did she have to
look to someone from England? Couldn't she see that I
could teach her all she needed to know? Usually a heavy
sleeper, I tossed most of the night, frustrated over the
inability of women to see things as logically as we men see
them.

The next day, after the evening meal, Erma approached
me with shining eyes. "Harry can give me time tonight," she
said. "The two of us will have to miss the evening meeting,
but I do need to counsel with him. He said he seldom
counseled with people in conferences like this, but he would
give me all the time I need."

I mumbled something about the goodness of God and
stalked away. This thing was growing worse. Dr. Prince spoke
that night, but I heard little of what he said. My eyes kept
wandering toward the side door, looking to see if Erma and
Harry would come sneaking in, their faces flushed with
excitement. They never showed up—which was worse.

After the meeting, Erma met us outside the auditorium.
Although I was about to burst with curiosity, I said nothing,
pretending that nothing had happened. We drove back to
the Raits' cottage, and Margie went straight to bed. Only
then did Erma open up.

"He asked me if I had been saved," she said.

I could have asked you that, I thought. But I said nothing,
just flipped through a magazine as though I were only
tolerating her enthusiasm.

"I told him I thought I had been saved when I joined the
Baptist church in West Stratford when I was nineteen."

That's not salvation, I thought.

"He told me that wasn't salvation," Erma rattled on, "and asked if I knew when I had been saved."

I poured myself some hot water and dipped a tea bag up and down, paying special attention to the coloring of the water.

"He knew I was floundering, so he asked me if I now believed that Jesus was the Son of God, and if I confessed Him as my Lord. When I said yes to both questions, he told me to write the date down in my Bible so I would never doubt again."

I looked up, and Erma's eyes were dancing with joy. "He then put his hand on my head and said a prayer. I felt a warm, wonderful feeling all over me."

How could I deny what she was saying? I thought. Here I am, sitting here and stewing in my jealousy while she is trying to tell me about the touch of God on her life. I was ashamed and reached over and touched her hand. How special she was to me.

"There's one more thing, Sherry," she said. "I want to be baptized again. This time I know it will be for real. Thirty years ago, I just didn't have any idea what it was all about. Now I want to be washed and begin all over again."

How well I understood her longing. A warm lovely glow came over me as I gripped her hand and prayed with her, in thanks for what God had done in her life that evening. I prayed, too, that there would be an opportunity for her to be immersed. And even though I didn't voice the words, I inwardly hoped that I would be the one chosen to perform the service.

A baptismal service was planned for the final session of the conference, Sunday afternoon, but we couldn't stay over. I was to speak at Harvest Temple in St. Petersburg Sunday night, and it would take most of the afternoon to drive the Tamiami Trail from Miami to the Tampa Bay area. Besides, there was a hurricane off the coast of Florida, and the waves had been extremely high. A baptismal service looked very remote for the time being.

Sunday dawned bright and fair, but the ocean was still fierce, the waves pounding the beach with thunder. However, we were told that the baptismal service would indeed be held following a communion service. Erma looked at me, and I nodded. Perhaps we could stay over and still make the meeting in St. Petersburg. For Erma, I would do anything.

The conference leaders asked if I would assist them. Remembering the pleasant time in the St. Simon's swimming pool, I gladly consented. It never occurred to me that my eighty-year-old legs might not be up to fighting the eight-foot waves.

We dismissed to the beach, and I hastily changed into my bathing suit and undershirt. Perhaps a score of persons had asked to be immersed, and the men who were to conduct the service took their places at the water's edge, while the huge congregation stood higher on the beach. Behind us was the pounding surf, almost drowning out the voice of Harry Greenwood as he stood, the foamy sea swirling around his ankles, and read from the Bible. There was a time of prayer, brief because the sky was rapidly turning dark as the offshore storm gave indication of moving upon us.

Then the candidates for baptism stepped forward, and at the head of the line was Erma. My heart leaped as she moved toward me, her head up, her eyes fixed on Jesus. The light on her face was the light of heaven, and I reached for her, only to have her brush by me as though I didn't exist, to be met at the edge of the water by the handsome Englishman, Harry Greenwood. Hand in hand, they walked into the swirling waters of the Atlantic and then, just as a giant swell loomed over them, I saw Harry lower her into the sea—"buried with Christ in baptism, raised to walk in the newness of life."

I moved toward them, but jumped back as the huge curl of the wave crested over me and crashed at my feet. I tried to rationalize that it was much better for Harry to perform the rite. I probably would have lost my footing, and both Erma and I would have been swept onto the beach gagging and sputtering in a very unspiritual posture. I timidly ventured out to help anyone who dared trust himself to my ministrations. Most of those coming, however, glanced at my frail body and the crashing waves and did what Erma had done, moved toward the stronger men. Floundering around in the waves, my eyes filled with salt and my mouth filled with water, I soon gave up and struggled up onto the beach where I sat exhausted, while the others finished the task. For the first time in months, I felt my age.

Two hours later, we were on our way to St. Petersburg. We arrived a full hour late, but the crowd—most of them, anyway—had waited. Erma and Margie were not among those who attended that delayed service, though. Margie was painfully tired, and Erma, still fresh as a spring flower from her marvelous experience in the ocean, eagerly volunteered to stay at the home of friends with her. Perhaps I could not hold my own with the younger men in the crashing surf, but when it came to preaching, I could go on all night. Indeed, after looking at my watch, I realized I had done almost just that. For ministering the Word, God had renewed my strength like the eagle.

It was good to be back in the front seat of the car with Erma at the wheel once more. Nearly two weeks had passed since we had returned from Florida, and Erma and I had managed to see each other every day. We were now on our way to New York State where I had been invited to speak at a meeting of the Full Gospel Business Men's Fellowship in Hornell. This would also afford me an opportunity to work in a visit with my son Bill and his family in Rochester, plus stopping by to see my sister, Leila, in Alexandria, Virginia, on our way back home. Margie went along so it would be "proper," for more and more Erma and I were realizing our futures together were meant for more than mere friendship.

We tried at times to include Margie in our conversation, but it was really as if our front seat was a different world from the back. I would glance over at Erma, our eyes would meet, and we would laugh uproariously at some gigantic secret jest. Often, when road conditions would permit it, she would drop her right hand from the wheel, and I would hold it tightly. It always thrilled me. A new confidence was growing in me, a sense of vigor and well-being which permeated my whole body. Never, even in my youthful days, had I felt the surge of love which throbbed in my veins and brought such excitement to my life. My second marriage had quickly evaporated into a relationship of tolerance. In fact, Thelma and I had usually occupied separate bedrooms. But as I contemplated a life together with Erma, it was more ecstasy than I could contain. I was back in my early twenties, remembering the joys I had looked forward to in those romantic days. Now with this new bond found in the baptism of the Holy Spirit, I foresaw that it would be even more breathtaking.

"Oh my Lord, You are too good to this old man," I prayed

silently. I could no longer doubt that the messages which
kept coming to me in the early hours of each day were truly
from God. He who ruled *my* life now ruled *our* lives also.
The growing conviction that we were destined to be man and
wife never left me.

As we drove on past the rolling hills of New York and
down the thruway toward Rochester, I began to regard Erma
more and more as actually my fiancée. What God had said to
me in one of the prophetic messages had made me feel we
were already each other's. In fact, that very morning, the
message in my quiet-time book had read:

> You are allowed, my child, to talk frankly to your bride-to-be
> about the advantages and disadvantages of marrying, as you
> now see them, but you are not to say one word of urging or
> pleading. I will attend to that.

We sped down the freeway in the gathering dusk. Rochester, and Bill's comfortable home, were still forty miles away.
Erma was beginning to tire. We had talked so animatedly for
hours that all three of us finally lapsed into silence.

Erma sighed. "I wish I had the gift of tongues," she said.
"Sherry, you say you often get all your energy back by
praying in the Spirit. I guess this is what Saint Paul meant
when he said that he who prays in tongues edifies himself.
How I wish I could do that right now."

I took her hand and began to pray out loud in tongues. I
could feel myself soaring, joyful, and almost immediately I
felt a response in Erma also.

"Keep it up, Sherry," she cried out, her eyes dancing. "I'm
getting new strength by the minute." My prayer turned into
singing in the Spirit. With a tremendous burst of new energy,

we sped on. It was as though the day itself had begun all over again.

Suddenly Margie called out from the back seat, "That was the Batavia exit we just passed while you two were doing all that rejoicing up there. We've gone too far."

She was right, and we had to drive on another eighteen miles before we could find another exit and reverse our direction. We were very late indeed for supper, but all was quickly forgiven when we arrived, bubbling over with the sheer exhilarating joy of the Lord. It was wonderful to discover that prayer in the Spirit could not only restore the soul and body of the one who prays—but overflow and give life to those around.

The FGBMFI meeting in Hornell the next morning was at the New Sherwood Hotel—how significant. I spoke for almost two hours—and could have gone on twice as long. I was embarrassed over my verbosity, but overjoyed at the power that surged through my ancient bones. I was not only in love—I was alive in Jesus.

In spite of what Erma and I both felt, we left my son Bill and his wife Rhoda on Sunday morning without telling them that Erma and I expected to be married. That announcement was left for my sister, Leila, and her husband, Carvel, who was a retired Brigadier General of the Marine Corps living in Alexandria, Virginia. By the time we arrived back in Charlotte, we were already making plans for a December wedding, although I had promised Leila that we would wait a while longer.

I hoped she would understand. After all, everyone knows that two kids in love never listen to reason.

5

Married in Haste

It was after midnight, and I had fallen asleep on my couch-bed when the telephone rang. Was it Erma? We had communed often over the phone for the last two weeks, looking forward to our wedding five weeks away. Instead of Erma, however, it was an old friend from Tampa, a Christian attorney.

"How would you like to go to Mexico with us this weekend?" he asked. "Three other couples are going to meet us in Guadalajara, and we need you along to introduce us to some Spirit-filled Christians."

My heart was pounding. If only this had waited five weeks. "Several married couples," he had said. Torn by the thought that the trip might set back our marriage until January, I promised to call him back the next morning, after I had talked to Erma. A plan was forming in my mind.

I hung up and sat pondering. Was this God's timing? I must have mused for the better part of an hour before giving way to the impulse and calling Erma's number. A sleepy voice answered. "I'll call mom," David said. Finally Erma came on the phone.

"Honey," I heard myself blurt out, "how would you like to get married this week and go to Mexico on a honeymoon?"

It was twelve hours later. Erma, Earle Barron, and I sat around the dining table in the living room of my apartment. Margie had cleared the table and was busy in the kitchen. We had been talking for almost two hours.

Earle, a local Presbyterian pastor and close friend, had just dropped by for a chat. We were using him as a sounding board for our questions.

"If you two are really going to get married anyway," Earle said, "perhaps the sooner the better!"

Erma gave a little smile. "My biggest concern has been my children. Nancy said only yesterday, 'Mom, I hope you are not confusing Sherry with Jesus.' Of course, I wish there were more time. The kids would like it to be a church wedding so they could take part in it. But . . . " Her voice trailed off, and she squeezed my hand.

Earle turned to me. "One thing bothers me, Sherry. If you and Erma get married, what are you going to do about your spiritual harem?"

I blinked in astonishment. "My what?"

"You have a following of widows and divorcées, as well as insecure married women. They flock to your prayer meetings and every one of them feels she has a vested interest in her minister-leader. Some of them will resent your marrying Erma—or any other member of that group."

I tried to dismiss the thought, but Erma laughed. "Earle knows too much about us women. We are like that. Perhaps the quicker we get this over and leave the country, the less painful it will be on your other female admirers."

I felt myself blushing, but I knew they were right. "Deane Ballard is arriving tomorrow," I said. "We want him to perform the ceremony. But we would have to leave the next day to meet our friends in Mexico, and that doesn't give us enough time to get a license."

"How about getting married in Mexico on arrival?" Earle asked.

"That's an idea. Bishop Saucedo is my good friend. He'd be glad to marry us. Yet we want Deane's blessing before we leave."

I called my friends Roger and Sally Noyes in Guadalajara. Roger was the treasurer of the diocese and was close to Bishop Saucedo. They were thrilled over our plans and agreed not only to arrange for the impromptu wedding, but to reserve a honeymoon room at the Mendoza Hotel near the cathedral.

Erma called our friend, Lucille Buening, in Charlotte, to make sure we could see Deane at her house the next afternoon. Somehow it seemed terribly important to us that Deane bless our marriage before we left for Mexico. In my own mind, this would make us married, for marriage is primarily a commitment to each other before God and in the presence of a representative of God's church. Having the blessing of Caesar (the state of North Carolina) seemed only incidental to having the blessing of God.

But the plan did not work out. Roger called back from Mexico. "We've struck a snag," he said. "The Mexican law requires a three-day wait, and you cannot have the religious service until you have had a civil service. Besides, the Bishop is leaving town the day after you arrive."

I was stunned, but recovered quickly, "Tell him we'll just have him bless our marriage. We'll have the real marriage here."

I knew what I had to do. I would ask Deane to marry us even though we did not have a license. After all, the honeymoon suite in Mexico was already reserved.

"Isn't that being disobedient to the civil law?" Erma asked with a raised eyebrow.

"I must obey God rather than man," I answered piously. But the question of timing still bothered me. I disliked being pressed, and disobeying the civil law did bother me, even though I refused to tell Erma. All I could hope for was the understanding of God.

I called my attorney friend in Tampa. "Prepare for a shock," I said. "I'll not only meet you in Guadalajara, I'll also introduce you to my new bride. You'll have one more married couple on your team." The die was cast.

When I asked my attorney friend how the trip was to be financed, he said, "The Lord will take care of all that, Brother Sherwood. Don't let the expense stop you."

In my euphoria, I took that as a promise he was going to pay the cost of my trip. After all, he had invited me, and I thought he knew I had no money. In fact, I had only enough money to buy two one-way tickets to Guadalajara. But believing he would reimburse me after we arrived, I was not over-anxious. What a honeymoon it promised to be!

Erma and I got to Lucille Buening's that Tuesday afternoon a few minutes before Deane arrived from the airport. We sat, waiting on the sofa in her den, our hands entwined. Deane arrived and listened to our story, hardly interrupting a single time. More than once he closed his eyes as though in prayer. Finally he nodded in assent, and fifteen

minutes later we were "married." "I, Sherry, take thee Erma
. . . to have and to hold, to love, cherish, and protect . . .
until Jesus comes again—or until one of us goes home to
Him. . . ." Of course, it was not legal, because we had no
license. But all of us were satisfied that God approved. I'd
take care of the legalities after we returned from Mexico.

I spent that night in the apartment with Margie while
Erma was home with her children, packing to go. The next
morning we were aloft. A golden haze hung over the city of
Charlotte and we sat by one another in the plane holding
hands. It was like a dream. That night we would check into
the Hotel Mendoza, and I would sleep with my bride.

Dusk was falling, and the high mountains that ringed the
airport near Guadalajara were in purple shadows as our plane
touched down. Two hours later, we had finished with the
blessing service at St. Mark's Episcopal Church. Even though
the bishop had been careful to point out that it was not a
wedding ceremony, we felt married—and that was all that
counted to me. We checked into our room at the hotel. We
had waited so long to consummate our love, and finally,
everything was in readiness. Everything, that is, except my
tired old body.

Erma stepped out of the bathroom dressed in a new sheer
nightgown. Our arms were around each other, and moments
later we were snuggled into bed. I switched out the lamp.

"I loved Jack so much," Erma said. "But I've been a widow
too long. That was another life. Now I can begin to live
again." I reached for her, my hands caressing. How eager I
was. But in spite of my great desire, my body failed to
respond.

I loved her so much. I held her so close. But that was all. I could do nothing else. I was an old man now, not a lusty young bridegroom. The moment of ecstatic anticipation faded into the cold realization that I was utterly unable to satisfy her fully aroused passion. Bitterly, I recalled my boasts made earlier. I was impotent.

"We are just too tired, Erma, sweetheart," I rationalized.

We slept, but only fitfully. I was ashamed. Embarrassed. And so unhappy for her. I wanted her to love me as a man, not just as a priest and father image. How I had longed for this night; now I longed for the day. Perhaps I could still make my bride happy if I showed her the sights of this beautiful city where my daughter and I had spent three such happy years.

But morning brought another form of disillusionment.

It was one of those beautiful days for which Guadalajara is famous. I started it singing in the Spirit as I went to the bathroom for my shower. As I emerged, Erma went in for hers. Moments later, she reappeared, a look of disgust on her face.

"Sherry, that whole floor is soaking wet. And all the hot water is gone. Did you really have to run the water so hard? Are you always so inconsiderate?"

I muttered some excuses and apologized, but deep inside I felt sick. I wanted her admiration as well as her love, but all I could merit was her scolding. Perhaps my sister was right. I had been a bachelor too long. My clothes were still left on the floor where I had kicked them off the night before. The bathroom was a mess, and I had been unable to satisfy my new bride. I was a miserable failure.

Sensitive to my need, Erma turned to me and held me close. Perhaps I had been wrong in thinking I could still perform as a young man, but I had not been wrong in my choice of a mate. Even though I was not who I thought I was, she was all I hoped her to be, and more. She understood. And the beautiful soft November sunshine, the pealing of the Cathedral bells, the shouts of the street vendors, and the delicious smells coming up toward our balcony window all combined to lift my spirits.

"I'll learn, honey," I whispered. "Just give me time."

The day passed quickly. Juan and Ingrid de Membrone, who had met Erma when on a trip to visit Margie and me last Easter, offered to show her one of the best curio and souvenir stores in the city. It frightened me to see the number of items piling up on the counter, to be checked off, wrapped, and sent over to the hotel. All too clearly I visualized my dwindling bank account back in Charlotte. Erma herself was disturbed when she saw what a large check I finally wrote but assured me the items would really save us money because they would make wonderful Christmas presents for friends back in Charlotte.

"Juan ought not to have encouraged me to buy so much," she protested. "And did you notice, Sherry, how he and that storekeeper were whispering in the corner? Juan gets ten percent on all the sales to customers he brings here. I almost wish I had not overheard them."

I agreed and comforted her further by reassuring her that our wealthy friends who had invited us on the trip would soon reimburse us for our plane tickets. What if we did spend all our money on curios? Additional funds would soon be coming so we could buy our return tickets home.

So if our Mexican honeymoon was proving a lot more expensive than I had anticipated, and if our lovemaking was practically nonexistent, the rest of the days still had their interests for us. There were sweet moments on the rooftop at sunset, when we shared a glass of sherry and watched the golden lights on the twin Cathedral towers. And the times with our friends who made up "the team," including our host from Tampa. With them, we were instrumental in getting a large group of Spirit-baptized people together and forming the first chapter of the Full Gospel Business Men's Fellowship in Guadalajara. God was blessing, in spite of my problems.

Guidance was badly needed, however, as it came time to leave. The team, including our host from Tampa, were going to Mexico City and Guatemala. They insisted that we go along, but we had run out of money. I kept waiting for my host to offer to reimburse us for our tickets and furnish money for our mounting hotel bill and our return flight, but he just smiled, clapped me on the back, and reassured us God would take care of everything. I wanted to be submissive, especially since we were their guests, so Erma and I decided the only thing to do was to ask Roger Noyes for a loan. We would go on to Guatemala and see how God led from there. We took Roger's willingness to help us as a sign from God to keep on traveling—despite the fact we were now down to our last fifteen dollars.

After another week in Guatemala, there was still no money forthcoming from my host. As in Mexico, a Full Gospel Business Men's Fellowship chapter had been organized as a result of our visit, and now the team decided to go on to Venezuela in South America. Once again they encouraged us to come along, saying God would take care of our expenses. By this time, however, it had become obvious that our host had no intention of helping us with our tickets home. He was indeed leaving that to God. Erma and I were in enough trouble already without going farther and farther away from home. At least we knew some people in Guatemala who would loan us some more money, and we knew no one in Venezuela. I had mental pictures of standing at the airport in Caracas while my friends boarded a plane back to Miami, leaving us behind with the encouraging words that we were not to worry, God would provide for us.

We told the team it was time for us to return home, borrowed money from two newly acquired Guatemalan friends, and flew back to Charlotte. We arrived with eleven dollars and sixty cents in our pockets, plus a couple of pesos and a few Guatemalan quetzals we'd brought back for souvenirs. I was in debt to friends in two countries and had totally depleted my Charlotte bank account. What a strange way to begin a marriage—this late in life.

Erma's children met us at the airport and dropped me off at my apartment. I gave my bride a hurried kiss and told her to call me in the morning. Here I was, back in the familiar apartment with my daughter, wondering if the entire honeymoon had not been just a dream—or perhaps more accurately, a nightmare.

6

Legal at Last

It was well toward noon before Erma called me that Wednesday morning after our return. I had not been anxious, being completely absorbed in preparing a circular letter to be sent to three hundred and fifty friends and relatives telling them of our marriage. While I was composing the letter, a very practical thought occurred to me. Why not suggest that instead of sending wedding gifts, they just send a check toward our travel expense to Mexico? It seemed a grand idea at the time, and it never occurred to me that everybody else, including Erma, would be horrified at my brashness.

"Sherry!" Erma's eyes were literally blazing as she looked up from the letter the next day. "You aren't really going to send this, are you?"

"What's the matter with it?" I argued, my voice weak and the palms of my hands moist. Of course, I already knew. I had goofed again. It seemed that after eighty years I would know better. Instead, I was getting worse.

"You're practically begging your friends for money. You

can't do that. I refuse to send any of these letters. I insist that
you do it over."

But it was too late. They were already in the mail, and my
puny efforts to defend my actions only made matters worse.
Erma was close to tears, and at last we just sat in silence, a
huge wall between us.

The phone rang, and while Erma was answering it, God
began to speak to me. Erma was right. Thank God I had a
wife honest enough to tell me where I was wrong—and to do
it in love. When would I ever learn to trust God and stop
walking around with my hand out?

The phone call was from Charlotte Hawthorne. Tom and
Charlotte, dear friends on the other side of the city, were
offering us their guest room in their big house. They knew we
were having to sleep apart because of the crowded conditions
of Erma's house. Their offer came as God's gift at a perfect
time. The walls were down as I apologized and explained to
our friends how wrong I had been.

Charlotte Hawthorne was easy to confide in. We reveled
in her happy, understanding interest. It was clear to her that
we needed a larger house. She reminded us that she had a
realtor's license, and she was quite sure she could locate a
suitable dwelling with a wing for Margie.

The following week, we accompanied Charlotte on a trip
to Columbia, South Carolina. While there, we decided not
to wait for Deane Ballard to return to North Carolina to
really marry us. Since there was no waiting period required in
South Carolina, we made up our minds to get our license and
legalize the marriage right away. We had waited long
enough.

That afternoon we found ourselves in a shabby room
before a cluttered desk in the state capital, waiting for a clerk

who could make out our license. Lighting a cigar and spitting into a receptacle beside the littered desk, the clerk leaned back and peered at us closely.

"So, you two want a license, do you? What kind? Fishing or hunting?" Then he gave an uproarious belly laugh at his stale joke, which I was sure he pulled on every couple who stood before him, and handed us two forms to fill out.

"Date of birth? Age?" I dutifully inscribed "October 14, 1889. Age: 80." The clerk looked hard at my answer, peered up at us, and then gave Erma a lecherous grin. I could read his thoughts and wanted to put my hands around his neck. I was in no mood for insults.

The papers were finally signed, and we were back out in the December sunlight. "What next?" I asked, hoping that Erma would come up with a positive suggestion.

"That's up to you," she said. "I only know I was within an inch of telling that man in there to forget the whole thing."

We felt better, though, after we rejoined Charlotte for the homeward trip. She was her usual cheerful, animated self. "Erma says you don't want to be married by a Justice of the Peace," she said. "We passed several churches on the way down from Charlotte. Since this is Wednesday night, I'm sure we'll find one open. That way you can have a church wedding."

"Yes," I mused, "if we can find some minister willing to marry us."

Almost as she spoke, we caught sight of a little church building by the side of the road. We were just outside Great Falls, South Carolina, a few miles from the state line.

"Church of God," the sign read. I knew the denomination, having spoken in Vep Ellis' Harvest Temple, a church of the same group, during our trip to Florida. The lights were just going on in the building, so Charlotte waited in the car while Erma and I knocked at the door of the parsonage next door.

The Reverend Mr. Gordon was kind, but aloof. It was not hard to read his thoughts. Here was this old man with a young woman on his arm, asking him to marry them on the spur of the moment. How could he know what he was getting into? Perhaps we were fugitives from the law. Maybe I was abducting her for white slavery. It could even be that we both had living partners and he was being asked to legalize our bigamy. He expressed his doubts, and Erma and I just stood before him, waiting in silence.

Suddenly I thought of something that might help. "Do you know Vep Ellis, a minister of your own denomination who has a church near St. Petersburg, Florida?" I asked. "He used to be Oral Roberts' song leader."

Pastor Gordon's eyes narrowed. "I know who he is; why do you ask?"

I told him I had preached in his church just a few weeks earlier and suggested he call him to verify who I was.

"That won't be necessary," the minister said, grabbing my hand and pumping it up and down. "I am a pretty good judge of character."

He was quite jovial now, calling out his wife and introducing her. "We are about to have our midweek service. Why don't you come next door and we'll conduct your wedding during the service? It will be a real treat for our people."

Ten minutes later, we were seated in the congregation, Charlotte beside us. Moments later, we were married—legally.

"Funny, I don't feel a bit different," Erma remarked as we left the building and headed north toward Charlotte. But we kissed a little harder than usual, and I felt a glow of renewed hope that now we would have better success with our intimate relations. Surely three marriages should patch things up splendidly.

"Sherry, how can we ever explain all these marriages to the prayer group? Who would understand?" Erma asked.

"We won't even try," I replied. "Let them think what they want."

Charlotte interrupted. "Wouldn't you two darlings like to spend the night at our house again? You can phone the children, Erma. They shouldn't mind."

My heart leaped. Another chance. Now, maybe I could make good as a bridegroom.

Erma squeezed my hand. I suspected her thoughts were the same as mine. Yet once we were in bed, I discovered that I had not, after all, suddenly found the fountain of youth for which I yearned. "Oh God, please make me ready," I prayed in my heart. But there was no answer.

It might well seem that a fourth marriage service would have been an anticlimax, but such was not the case. Deane Ballard, of course, was somewhat puzzled when we told him the following Tuesday evening that we had already had a legal ceremony, but we wanted him to perform still another blessing service. We had reserved the Moravian Chapel, and it was well-filled the night of the final ceremony.

Only a few knew that Deane had held a service for us before we left Charlotte. Fewer knew we had been "married" in Mexico, and almost no one knew of the wedding the week before in the little church beside the road in South Carolina. Therefore all present were happily thrilled with the beauty of the service in the little chapel. Erma looked so beautiful in her new dress. Nancy was very lovely, a sparkling-eyed little

bridesmaid for her mother. All our worries and doubts that
we might have somehow failed God by our manner of
marrying were at last put at rest. Surely after four wedding
ceremonies, we were as married as anyone could be. Now all
I had to do was ask God to turn me into a gentleman who
didn't eat like a horse or splash water all over the bathroom,
take away my financial insecurity, and restore my fading
potency.

As I sat there half dreaming, half waking in that chair
beside the battered old desk, reliving the past five weeks in all
their poignancy, I began to pray again as I had early that
morning after our quarrel.

"Dear God, work a miracle in our lives. Let me become
the man she thinks she married. Let her find joy in this
marriage that seems so frightfully incomplete right now. Let
us really begin again, and not in vain. That way, it will be all
to Your glory."

My prayer was sincere. Only a miracle could pull us
through.

7

Prince Charming Rides Again

Someone slammed the apartment door, and I jerked wide awake at the desk. Margie was back from her new job as Archer Torrey's secretary at Christ Church. I blinked back to reality.

I had been dozing in the rickety Morris chair in front of the scuffed old oak desk. I had told Erma I was going to return to the apartment to write some letters. The correspondence was piled high on the desk. But even though it was not yet noon, my old body refused to stay awake. I glanced at my watch. For three hours all I had done was sit and doze—reliving those weeks of disillusionment and frustration.

Margie's cheerful voice reminded me that I was still living in two worlds. I had been a widower for a long time with Margie as my only companion. Now I was married, to a woman younger than my daughter. Yet even after four wedding ceremonies, I still felt more comfortable with Margie than with Erma. Had I made a mistake? Perhaps the three of us were to live together? But what of Erma's three

teenagers? And then there was Margie's criticism of Erma's
housekeeping. I looked at the stack of unanswered mail on
the desk, remembered the arguments Erma and I had had
during the night, and muttered, "You're an old fool, Bill.
Why did you ever get married?"

Had my black thoughts last night been partly right? Had I
deeply wronged Erma by persuading her into a marriage
which really might not have been guided by God after all?
What proof had I that all those prophecies I had received—
the ones promising me virility and Margie happiness—were
from the Lord? Was the whole thing an illusion?

"Lord, show me," I prayed.

The phone interrupted my self-pity. I felt my heart leaping
and pounding as Erma's voice flowed over the wire. Impotent or not, I was very much in love. "Erma," I swallowed,
"honey, I've missed you like crazy."

She was giggling. "But it's only been three hours."

"I know," I said, fighting to keep from sounding like a silly
teenager. "We fight like cats and dogs when we're together,
and yet we can't bear to stay apart. I really do need you
around."

I could hear her breath on the other end of the line, and
felt a burning in my loins. Maybe there was hope for me yet.

A half hour later, Erma stood at the door of the study. I
had not even heard the outer door open and close. How
radiant she looked! Again I was whispering a thank You to
the Lord whose love had united us. It all felt so real, and the
close hard squeeze and hug we gave one another, the moist
kiss as our lips met, confirmed that the flame had not gone
out, not yet, in my old body. I quite forgot that Margie was
standing in the door looking on. Well, at least she knows we
are really married now.

Margie left to fix lunch, and I stood looking at Erma. "Honey, I'm not old. I just seem to have a few old-age symptoms, that's all."

Erma's eyes sparkled. "Beautiful. You're not a skinny old man and I'm not a chubby, middle-aged woman. Inside I'm a tall, willowy blonde, and you're a young Prince Charming."

How I loved her at that moment. It was even better than it had been on the telephone. Why couldn't it always be just like this?

"Sherry," Erma said seriously, "maybe you don't believe in God as much as you think you do."

I looked at her through squinted eyes. I knew she was leading up to something honest, and I was afraid. Yet we had promised to "speak the truth in love." I licked my drying lips and nodded for her to go on.

"I've told you before that my kids think you're a big phony—" She paused, not wanting to hurt, I knew, but compelled to be honest. "Sherry, are you a phony?"

I knew all the arguments. I had used them for years. But they all seemed so empty in the face of her love.

"I'm not sure anymore," I stammered. "Maybe I am. Maybe I'm all front, like an old movie set."

"Do you want to be real?" Erma asked. My heart was pounding. I had dreaded this showdown with reality. My former parishioners had been intimidated by my clerical collar and priestly position. No one had ever forced me to face myself. After all, a priest is supposed to have all the answers. That I had been empty for years had either gone unnoticed by others or, if observed by others, was simply neglected as a fact of life. My two former wives had drifted into a relationship with me where tolerance of my bad habits, phoniness, and shallow thinking had become a way of

existence. My first wife had seen my need and had cared
enough to try to show me. Perhaps my stubborn resistance to
change had been the real cause of the crippling arthritis of
her later years. But no one had ever loved me enough to dig
as deeply into my soul as Erma seemed compelled to do.

"I'm afraid," I said slowly. "Afraid that you'll peel me like
an onion and find, when you finish, that there isn't anything
at the center. Sometimes I think I'm like that fictional
character who came into town and made such a good
impression, but when he was run over by a carriage, they
discovered he was filled with sawdust." I dropped my head.
"Maybe I am a phony. I really thought I loved and trusted
God, but maybe I don't. But . . . I know I want to."

"Thank You, God," Erma breathed, squeezing my hand.
"That is what I've been waiting for you to say, Sherry. Praise
God, for once you aren't trying to prove you are right. All
that bragging before we were married about your virility.
What difference does it make? You don't have to prove
anything to me."

I thought back to those early morning hours when I had
pulled away from her, angry because I couldn't make myself
into the kind of lover boy I thought I was. She was right. I
was proud. Too proud. Yet even stripped of my facade by her
love and honesty, I still groped about for some remnant to
hide the shame of my nakedness. What could I say, even
now, to convince her that I really was a man? After all, if I
couldn't perform sexually, then how could she ever believe in
me as a man? And if she couldn't believe in me as a man,
how could she accept me as a priest?

I thought back to my second wife, Thelma, and how we
had just drifted apart into separate bedrooms. Thelma never
really enjoyed sex, nor expected it. As I grew older, it was

easy to simply stop thinking about it. But Erma was different. Still young, passionate, her body yearned to be fulfilled. Yet look what she had picked to fulfill her. An impotent old man. God, what a mess.

We were both silent now. Would I ever be able to make good as a husband? As a lover? At eighty, had I passed the point of no return? I groped for the rickety old chair, intending, perhaps, to sit down and go back to sleep. I was interrupted by Erma's musical laughter.

"What's funny, honey?" I asked without expression.

"What's funny, honey?" she teased, mocking me. "Why, you're funny, Sherry. Why else would I marry you? Because you're the sex symbol of the wheelchair set? You've forgotten I fell in love with you long before we ever crawled into bed together. Perhaps you were sitting around drooling, waiting for the moment when you could exhibit your prowess as a young lion. But sex isn't everything, Sherry. Real love is ever so much more important—if you have to choose. But we can change. If you really believe in God as much as you say you want to, with God's help you can perform as a man. I know you can. Anyway marriage is based on love, not sex. Would you love me if I were confined to an iron lung? Would I love you if you were locked away in some prison and all we could do was rub noses through the bars? Of course. We've something the younger kids don't have, sweetheart, we have love. And furthermore, I believe we'll have a wonderful sexual union when you let God totally renew your body. He *can*, you know!"

A wave of thankfulness swept over me. Erma was right. Praise God for her honesty. I felt warm and loving again, as though God were smiling on us. I reached out and pressed her hand, that delicious soft warm hand that had thrilled me so as we had driven all those miles when our love was budding, blossoming in our veins. I pulled her to me, thanking God for the truth He had revealed that I didn't need to prove myself sexually in order to be a man—or a husband.

Yet as I buried my face in the curve of her neck, I heard God's still small voice whispering, *That's right, Sherry, but with Me all things are possible. Trust Me—and keep trying.*

I found myself agreeing, making resolutions. I'll start really working toward that, I thought. I haven't even talked to a doctor yet. I've been too ashamed. But I will. There may be pills, or special vitamins. More protein in my diet. Maybe exercise will help. I need to start my jogging again. I'll get there. By God's help—

Desire was back, strong and virile. "Now," I whispered, "right now, I bet I could really make good as your husband."

Erma chuckled and kissed me lightly. "It's noon, lover, and Margie has lunch ready. Bedtime's a long way off."

I was battling again. John and I were to work on the household bills tonight, and then he would want his own bed. Erma would probably sleep on the couch, and I'd wind up back here at the apartment. I headed for the kitchen and lunch. All my old friends were either dead or in nursing homes. Perhaps they were the fortunate ones after all. At least they didn't have to try to prove they were something they weren't.

8

Too Old to Begin Again

I had known John White, Erma's twenty-two-year-old son, before I knew any other member of my new family except Erma herself. In fact, it was John with his great need for healing prayer who had really brought us together in the first place. Handsome, lovable, and very happy about our marriage, John had been forced to assume the business headship of the home after his father died. But much as I loved John, grateful as I was for his continued improvement from leukemia, I certainly didn't look forward to spending this particular evening in his company, paying the household bills.

"Why did you have to pick out this night of all nights?" Erma asked as she wandered restlessly back and forth from the kitchen to the living room. She was as disturbed as I. Both of us had other ideas on how the evening should be spent.

"It really has to be," I replied, as firmly as I knew how. This was the first time we had been able to find time to look at the bills, some of them considerably overdue. John had been away. He usually attended to them the first of the month. But this month had been different. I had secured a thousand-dollar loan to pay back the money I'd borrowed from the friends in Mexico and Guatemala. I had about three hundred of it left plus about half of my month's retirement income after paying the bills that had accumulated in the apartment during my absence—which included a terrific telephone bill with calls to Mexico and New York. John had received his disability allowance from the Navy that week and added it to my own resources.

Now we couldn't even find a place to work. Every table or flat surface in the little living room was completely occupied —piled high, overflowing with school books, papers, magazines, odds and ends. It was just like every drawer and closet shelf in Erma's house—all overflowing. Finally John came up with a card table, and we pulled up two chairs. "Let's get going," he said brashly. I meekly obeyed.

"Here are all the bills I can find," John said. "There will be a few more coming in, but you can let them go till some time in January. You write the checks, and I'll address envelopes and lick stamps."

We set to work. John called off the debts and suggested amounts that we would pay. I set the figures down and added them up. My heart sank lower and lower. The thousand dollars I had borrowed from the bank in St. Petersburg where I had my little trust fund suddenly shrank into pitiful inadequacy. I'd already had to dip into it to pay the month's rent for my apartment—not to mention the electric light bill and the phone bill. My head was whirling as I looked at the mounting list in front of me. There were two phones in this little house; John and Erma had separate listings. Like mine in the apartment, each of the bills was swollen with long-distance calls. Here was the Duke Power bill—how could an electric bill be that large?

"That's really for two months," John explained. "We're lucky they didn't cut the power off." The same was true of the double water bill. "These must be paid in full, and quick," he said.

There was a sheaf of department store bills—Belk's, Penney's, Zayre's, Eckerd's. And then the Park Road Drug Store. "And what's this one, John? Do you really still owe four hundred dollars on The World's Greatest Books?"

John explained it was only fifteen dollars a month. "Probably for the rest of our lives," I muttered. "But don't worry. At this rate, none of us will live very long."

Then John handed me the gasoline company bills. There was Humble and Shell and Sun Oil and Gulf . . . I tried to be funny. "How come you folks don't have a Texaco card?"

"We do," John replied seriously. "But we haven't used it for the last few months. I think we are paid up. Oh no, here's their old bill. We'll have to pay something on that, too."

Then came the credit-card companies. The simplicity of my life in Mexico, where I paid cash for everything, had kept me ignorant of Mastercharge and BankAmericard.

"That's all right," John assured me. "We don't have to pay the full amount. Ten percent of the current balance will keep our credit good with them. This is one for two hundred and eighty-four dollars, so we only have to pay thirty dollars. This other one, well, you'll have to write a check for forty dollars."

I studied the itemized bills for a few minutes. "But John," I said, "do you realize that we have to pay eighteen percent annual interest on all the unpaid balance? That's unheard of. We can't do that."

"This is modern living, Sherry," John countered. "Where have you been all this time? Haven't you ever carried credit cards?"

Just for gasoline, I thought. And I've believed I had to pay those bills in full every month. I've never paid any interest of any kind, and here I've married into a family that is living off credit cards, and going deeper and deeper into the hole each month. I shuddered. There was nothing ahead but disaster. Sheer disaster. I saw no way out.

"These credit cards come in pretty handy," John rattled on. "Right now, with Christmas coming up in less than two weeks, what would we do if we didn't have them? I've been thinking of applying for a couple more. Perhaps American Express and Diner's Club." John looked a little wistful as he said it. He loved living "high on the hog," and he'd had so little opportunity.

I wondered about John. Did he share his mother's confident faith that God was really healing him? Or, with his medical training, did he accept the doctor's prognosis that his leukemia was only in "deep remission" and would one day return? I knew how he yearned to travel, and to spend money. What was really going on behind those blue eyes with their look, sometimes so far away, sometimes so piercingly near?

I did not argue with him about the credit cards. Perhaps I was too naïve, too ignorant of this modern world. I picked up the bills we had already listed when suddenly I realized that each one of these, too, was carrying an eighteen percent interest charge on the unpaid balance. I dropped them on the table as if they were on fire.

"Good heavens, John!" I exclaimed. "This family is paying out many hundreds of dollars a year in unnecessary interest charges, not to mention going deeper and deeper into debt each month. Can't we get on a cash basis?"

John ignored my feeble protest. "Here's the insurance bill for $184. And the car payment for $175, for which we're a month behind also."

My head was swimming. "John, that's a terribly high car payment, isn't it? It's almost twice as much as anything I ever had to pay."

"Well, frankly, Sherry, it's twice as much car as you've been used to."

Of course he was right. It had been three years since I'd owned a car at all. Ever since my car and that Mexican bus had met at an intersection in Guadalajara, I had been satisfied to walk, ride buses, or travel around with friends. That was one of the reasons I found Mexico such a desirable place to live on my retirement income—I didn't need a car. But of course, in America, everyone drives. Or gets run over by those who do.

I sighed and looked up at John. "And then there's the land deal," he said. "That's one payment we must make each month. It's $315."

I almost choked. "Land deal?"

"Sherry, this is the most important thing on the whole list. This is our one hope of getting out of this financial mess. Mom and all us kids have a stake in it. We just can't afford to let it go."

His intensity scared me. I was afraid to ask for more, fearing what would come. But he told me anyway.

"It's a first-class land development in the Pocono Mountains of Pennsylvania, just near enough to New York to have a tremendous future. It will have everything, including a club with a golf course, recreation, swimming pools, tennis, everything. It's beautiful country. Woods all around. There will be good roads into it . . ."

"There *will* be?" I almost shouted. "You mean there aren't any roads into it now?"

"Well, no, not yet. But the agent said they're moving fast."

My heart was sinking. I had heard it all before, a hundred times, from naïve parishioners who had bought swamps in Florida, nonexistent islands off the coast of California, desert gullies in Texas. All had been promised that this would be a thriving paradise—one day. Such developments were usually sold sight unseen after the buyer had been suckered into the scheme by a fast-talking salesman who had beautiful color brochures showing how the land would look—one day. How well I remembered the old joke so often told down in Brownsville, Texas, where one realtor said to another, "You know, Jim, all those lies we used to tell about this land have come true."

I knew it could happen. Maybe one day they would build a road into the Poconos and there would be tennis courts and golf courses where now there was nothing . . . but I knew the terrifically high odds against it.

So this was the investment John was counting on to get him out of debt. Even as he talked, I detected clearly that secret, hidden fear—that the remission in his leukemia was only a temporary thing.

"John, are you sure this land development company is really legitimate?"

My words sounded so lame. In my heart, I knew the more than two thousand dollars this little family had already paid into the scheme was down the drain. And now I was to be responsible for sending another $315 swirling after it.

"It's a good company," John said, his voice soft now. "It's only a question of time before we'll all be rich. Besides, you see, I couldn't buy insurance—" He left the sentence hanging. I understood.

"But suppose you miss a payment or two," I quizzed. "What sort of contract do you have with those people?"

"Frankly, Sherry, that's what bothers me. We're a little late on the last payment, and we've got to make it even if we let everything else go. They can cancel the whole contract on us if we miss even one month."

I groaned. I had married into this?

I heard John's words out of the fog, bringing me back to reality. "Sherry, are you aware that we had to send back mom's Social Security check? She won't be getting it any more now she is married again."

I had difficulty taking it in. The thought of last night came back to me. "No fool like an old fool." The devil was chuckling in my ear. All I had was an irrevocable trust fund down in St. Petersburg. I had it fixed that way ten years ago when a small inheritance came my way. My lawyer knew I was a fool for a soft touch and would probably give away all the principal if I could get at it. So, showing me how important it was to have a steady income in my old age, he had persuaded me to lock it up. Only I never knew I would live this long, nor that I would try to start all over again at eighty by marrying a woman so deeply in debt we'd all wind up in the poorhouse.

Erma stormed past the table. "Can't you ever think of anything but money, Sherry? Can't you trust God one little bit?"

The unfairness of the attack stung, and I saw red. Grimly trying to control my voice, I said, "Please, let us alone.

We've got to finish this job. We've got all these checks to write and can't get anywhere if you keep butting in."

I had risen to my feet and was actually shouting. Erma and I were facing each other like fighting game cocks. John caught the excitement and began to shout, too. With the two of us ganging up against her, Erma made a face and retreated to the kitchen.

Almost panting from my effort to control my inner rage, I turned back to the task of actually writing the checks. It hurt, watching the little balance dwindle and finally die out in a wreath of zeros. Erma was all too right about one thing. I did have an inordinate love of hanging on to money. And she, I thought grimly, had an equal yearning to get rid of it.

I helped John put away the card table and get rid of the debris—those gaily printed slips that came with each bill, urging us to buy even more luxury items. Oh, this modern civilization. It had been so much easier to economize back fifty-five years ago when I had married my first wife and we had set up housekeeping on less than $100 per month in our little rectory.

True, the value of money had changed also. Back then, I never felt I was poor and I had never been in debt. If we couldn't afford it, we didn't buy it. I felt a surge of hatred for credit cards, the very tools of Satan. How would Erma and I ever get together in this matter of spending money?

For the moment, the incompatibility in our attitude towards finances completely dwarfed the nagging frustrations of our sex life. And, irony of ironies, I suddenly learned that we were to sleep together tonight after all. Nancy had told her mother that she was going to spend the night with her friend Mary Lou next door. "You and Sherry can have my bed again." A few hours earlier I would have rejoiced at this reprieve from having to return to my apartment across town. Now, I almost wished I were safely over there in that quietness and peace.

Erma was nearly asleep as I crawled in beside her, but she did whisper to me as I brushed her forehead in a perfunctory kiss. "Sherry, don't be too disgusted with us. We never used to get in debt in the old days when Jack was living. We paid cash for everything. It's just been lately . . . with John so sick . . . I couldn't bear it to deny the kids anything. . . ."

She trailed off into sleep and I kissed her again with a rebirth of love. But she was too sleepy to make any response; and my head, as I tried to say my last evening prayer, was just a jumble of dollar signs and figures. Maybe Satan was right. Maybe I was just too old to begin again.

9

A New Direction

The kids overslept their alarm the next morning. I wakened and looked at my wristwatch. Could it possibly be seven-thirty already? The house was still dark and silent. Erma and I roused the young people, bullied them through a hurried dressing, got them safely in and out of the bathroom and off to school. Only John remained, still fast asleep after last night's struggle with the bills.

"Get back in bed, Sherry!" Erma pleaded. "The house is cold. Brrr. I'll be with you in a minute." She yawned, stretched once or twice, and somehow, without a bit of makeup, managed to look more desirable in my eyes than I had ever seen her up to that minute. All my worries of the previous night concerning imminent financial disaster melted away.

Giggling and squirming, Erma snuggled up against me. "She squiggles," I thought to myself. We lay very still now, happy to be in one another's arms, all barriers gone. I prayed aloud. "Oh Father God, we thank You for this hour."

Erma murmured her assent, and at the same time I felt her

warm hand on my chest. I knew she could feel the throbbing of my heart. I started to turn toward her when the interlude was interrupted by the jangling telephone in the hall.

Erma mumbled something which didn't sound too spiritual, untangled herself from the sheets, and hurried into the hall to get the phone. Moments later, I heard her shouting.

"Sherry, get on the extension. It's Charlotte Hawthorne, and she wants us to come to a special meeting of the prayer group this morning. Tell her we can't make it. She won't believe me."

But I was simply incapable of telling Charlotte Hawthorne any such thing. "Darlings," her soft voice came over the wire, "please come. It's at ten. We need you."

I somewhat weakly assured her we'd be there and hung up.

"Sherry! Why did you say that? Don't you want to come back to bed with me?" Erma was standing in the door with her hands on her hips, a look of dismay in her eyes.

"But honey, we simply can't pass up all the group meetings. They are our friends. They are counting on us." My protests sounded so hollow, and were entirely contrary to my real desires. Yet to cover my selfishness, I argued even louder, and for ten minutes, Erma and I paced through the bedroom, yelling at each other. Finally, Erma gave way to silence and started to dress. Even if we had agreed to stay home, our desire had been quenched by the disagreement.

In the car, we sat in stony silence, carefully polite, avoiding a real quarrel. Arriving at Sarah Tomlinson's house, we entered the front door without knocking, and we caught them in a state of embarrassment. Obviously, the women had been talking about us, animatedly, just before we entered. Now they clammed up. Some of them wouldn't even look at us.

Several new faces were in the group, and introductions
were made. "This is our honeymoon couple," someone
quipped. "They're just back from— Where was it you went,
Erma?" But the woman didn't even wait for the answer
before rattling on about something else. Earle Barron's
arrival at the meeting served to remind me of his prior word
of warning about offending my "spiritual harem" by marrying Erma. Was jealousy the cause of this icy reception?

I forced myself to snap out of this line of thinking. What a
way to start a prayer meeting. Forgive me, Lord.

I found the group really did want to pray, however. They
settled down to the real business that had brought them
together and prayed with deep sincerity. There were many
needs. One woman prayed feelingly for a friend with
terminal cancer of the uterus. Another rather timidly asked
prayer for a home where the husband had a bad drinking
problem and the children were going hungry. Still another
spoke of a marriage about to break up because of another
woman. I wished we did not have to hear quite so many of
the sordid, depressing details. How I wished that some of
these dear women would not be quite so specific with the
Lord. As usual, I blundered into prayer two or three times
when someone, praying rather softly, was not quite through.

"Lord, heal these eighty-year-old ears of mine, or at least
give me more discernment to know what's going on," I
prayed after interrupting for the third time. Then I added a
postscript to the prayer. "Or, tell these ladies to speak up
when they pray."

I looked at Earle. Perhaps he was the reason God had
prodded us out of our warm bed this cold morning. Erma
and I obviously needed counsel from a qualified minister. I
decided to speak to Earle as soon as the meeting was over,

but before I could get to him, Erma got to me. From between clenched teeth, she whispered, "It's bad enough having all these women look at me like the third person in a triangle. Why do you have to be such a jackass when you are with them? Sherry, you are an old goat. Can't you control that show-off spirit? It's like a regular demon. You tell everybody else to learn to sit quietly, yet the instant there is a moment of silence, you blurt out some nonsensical utterance. And once you start speaking, you can't stop. I'm mortified."

For once I made no effort to defend myself. I was all too conscious of how exactly her description fit my problem. It seemed all I could do when I got into a meeting was rattle on and on. Not only was I an impotent old man, I was a compulsive talker. I needed help.

Two hours later, Earle and I sat relaxed in the study of my apartment. Erma had dropped me off and then gone on with her daughter Nancy to do some Christmas shopping. Margie was at work, and Erma had promised to return by suppertime, so I wasted no time getting into my problem.

"I'm older than I thought I was," I sighed. "I simply cannot satisfy Erma's needs. I have plenty of passion, but I can never perform."

I felt color coming into my cheeks. Why, I wondered, was it so hard for me, even after two marriages, to speak out plainly? I thought I had discarded prudishness, especially with a close friend like Earle. But here it was, cropping up again.

I waited for Earle's reaction, not knowing whether he would be offended, would burst out laughing, or would call me a dirty old man and storm out of the room. "Go on," Earle said kindly.

Breathing easier, I moved ahead. "Just at the minute she's the readiest, I fizzle out. Then I can't seem to get started again. I'm all fuse and no explosion. And then, because I know I have failed, I take it out on her. She reacts, and we wind up shouting at each other in bed. I guess the truth is, Earle, I am just a dried up old man. I never should have tried marriage at my age."

Earle sat for a few moments in thoughtful silence. "Tell me one thing, Sherry. Do you feel frustrated because you can't perform sexually, or are you frustrated for a different reason?"

I hung my head. "I guess my days of enjoying sex are over—and have been for some time. My second wife and I married mostly for companionship, and we usually slept in separate rooms. I love Erma, however, as a young man does his bride. Before marriage, I bragged to her of my virility. I was sure God had revitalized me sexually. But I'm dried out."

Earle's eyes were boring into me. "Sherry, I'm going to do exactly what Erma has been doing. I am going to speak the truth in love. Your impotence is not so much due to your old age, as to the fact that you have never felt sex was quite right in God's sight, or that it mattered to your partner whether or not significant sexual activity occurred. In truth, Sherry, you've always been dried up on the inside, even when you were young. That's the reason you felt so compelled to boast of your virility beforehand and now to prove yourself to be manly."

I was battling now as Earle suggested I change, not my methods, but my attitude toward sexual relationships. I knew he was right. I had always built dream castles and set them up as goals. Then, when I was unable to achieve, I would withdraw into the frustration of failure. It was easier with Thelma to move into separate bedrooms on the pretext of growing old, than to face and overcome the problems causing our poor relationship.

Earle continued. "But Sherry, you don't have to remain as you are. Men are not like old dogs who cannot learn new tricks. Men are God's marvelous creation and even at eighty—or should I say especially at eighty—you are capable of learning. You have been baptized in the Holy Spirit which opens you to new truth. No longer do you need to be locked into the bondage of the past. Now you can attempt a real relationship with a real woman—one who will not only speak truth to you, but will stimulate you as well. No, sex is not your problem, Sherry. Your impotency is not in your organs, it is in your spirit. Let God touch your spirit, and your body will respond also."

Ashamed, I sat quietly. I knew he was right, and it was time for this old man to take a new look at his relationship with Erma—and God. What a prudish, moralistic old idiot I had been. I nodded my head. I would take Earle's counsel as the word of God for my life. Indeed, even as I considered it, I felt a flush in the pit of my stomach. Perhaps this was just the release I had been waiting for, and with it would come new energy for my body also. I knew I was not impotent, just bound by the chains of tradition. I glanced at my watch, eager for Earle to leave so I could shave and shower and be prepared for Erma when she came for me. Yes, tonight would be the night.

But as Earle left, the phone was ringing. It was Erma. "You'd better spend the night there at the apartment," she said. "Margie really needs your company, and Nancy and I still have some shopping to do. I'll come by in the morning."

I slumped back in the old chair. Defeated. Would I never achieve again?

10

The Last Word

I sat on the low bench in front of the fire I had just rekindled in the living room. It was 3:00 A.M. and my back hurt so badly I couldn't sleep. An eighty-year-old man has no business attacking a dead tree with a saw.

Erma was sound asleep in John's room. I was glad I hadn't wakened her when I stumbled out of bed in the pitch dark. It had been almost a month since my talk with Earle, but I was still in bondage, and with this pain in my back, lovemaking was out of the question. Besides, the situation had grown so bad between Erma and me that we were now simply struggling to keep the marriage together, with no thought of making progress.

The news that one of the women in the prayer group had publicly requested prayer for our "faltering" marriage hurt almost as bad as my back. Why did they have to be so specific in their prayers in that group? Why couldn't she just have requested prayer for "Sherry and Erma who aren't able to be with us today?" Why did she have to blab to all those women that we were having roaring arguments and our marriage was faltering? And then, to have to get the news of her announcement through the grapevine, which seemed to be flourishing so strongly in Charlotte.

Yet the fact it was now public knowledge did not sting so much as the fact our marriage did need prayer. It was *not* working out. In fact, there was good evidence our matrimonial ship was sinking, and no amount of time on the pumps seemed to be keeping it afloat. Every day the waterline was higher. It seemed to be just a matter of time until there would be nothing left but bubbles—and debris.

Which Erma do I love? I wondered, as I poked at the embers in the fireplace. The physical Erma who lives in that plump but lovely body—or was it the Erma who liked to minister beside me, yet who laughed all too easily at things I could not think were funny. Then there was the frightened little girl Erma. I'd seen more of that Erma lately, usually after one of our increasingly frequent and violent quarrels.

There had been a bad moment when she slapped my face and I slapped back. Then I grabbed her and held her to me so tightly I actually hurt her rib cage. I knew I wanted to hurt her. I loved her and I hated her. She had not resisted. She had simply gone limp and said coldly, "Have you had enough now, Tarzan? I like men who are strong, but strong like Jesus."

"Damn!" I shouted, and stalked out of the house. I walked rapidly for blocks that morning, trying to stomp out my anger. I tried to pray, but the words would not come, even in tongues. When I returned to the house, I had forgotten the subject of our argument, which surely is one of the *assets* of old age. But there were always new subjects. In fact, every subject in our lives became the basis of a quarrel.

"What divides us is always money, or Margie," Erma

complained. Margie herself was probably as ignorant of this as the money was. But the fact remained that either subject had overtones which made Erma see red.

I was equally disturbed by Erma's preoccupation with her son, John, who seemed to me far too healthy for her constant sympathy and coddling. Then there was Erma's absolute disregard of the value of money, and her resentment of what she called my stingy, beggarly attitude. I knew I had a tendency to be extravagant, and I had repeatedly fallen for the appeals of a slick salesman. I could not be safely turned loose in a good bookstore, nor in a hardware store either. But I was aware of my shortcomings and I tried to keep my spending under control.

Erma, however, was almost any storekeeper's dream, and she seemed not to realize that everything she bought would have to be paid for sooner or later. Christmas had been a dread to me, for I knew from all the packages coming into the house that this little family was going way over the limit. I groaned daily as I thought of the credit cards and charge accounts that made it unnecessary for them to hold back when anything took the fancy of mother or sons or daughter. As a consequence, I held my own Christmas shopping down to the lowest limits and ended by buying my bride a box of candy and some writing paper—two of the worst things I could have picked out. She never wrote letters (resentful of the fact that I wrote all the time) and with her weight problem, giving her candy was like pouring gasoline into this smoldering fireplace in front of me. As usual I wound up eating the candy myself.

Between Christmas and New Year's, the tension had gotten so tight that I seriously considered going back to my apartment for a while. When I mentioned this to Erma, she lashed out violently, her eyes blazing as she shouted harshly.

"Go on back and live with Margie. That's where you really belong. You're just alike."

Then, as suddenly as it had begun, the fight left her. She collapsed, sat on the edge of the bed and pressed her hands over her eyes as she shook with dry sobs. Taking her hands down, she looked at me like a little frightened girl.

"Sherry, don't leave me. You are the only hope I've got. I need you."

I knelt beside her, and her arms crept around me, holding me tight against her breast. At that moment, I knew I loved her dearly and could never think seriously of leaving her. Yet it was not the love of a husband I seemed to feel, rather that of a father with his little girl. It was as though she had crept up into my lap with a bleeding finger and said, "Kiss it, daddy." Erma needed me, perhaps even more than my own daughter ever had.

I kissed her forehead, her cheeks, tasting the salty tears, and said, "We'll begin again. Luvaluia."

She squeezed me tighter and whispered, "Oh yes. Luvaluia! Count it all joy. We'll try harder."

But this last quarrel had been different. There had been new overtones, stirred as before by my insecurities. Even though Erma and I were married—indeed four times married—I still had not entered into that state of union where "two become one." Simply saying vows does not bring two people into unity. Nor does sleeping with your wife make two one. Our bodies could come together, however imperfectly, but oneness of thought, oneness of soul, was something that still eluded us. The fact that I had even considered walking away from Erma was evidence of our still unmarried souls. And the fact I was still capable of jealousy was even greater proof of my insecurity—for jealousy is founded on fear, the fear of losing something that is yours. In true marriage, people don't belong to each other—they *are* each other. And that was yet to be accomplished in our lives.

At a New Year's Eve party, we had bumped into an old friend of mine whom Erma had not yet met. Richard King was tall, handsome, and about Erma's age. He was the man Charlotte Hawthorne had once told Erma about—long before our marriage.

"He may be the answer to your prayer to find a Christian husband," Charlotte had said. "He told some in the prayer group that he is looking for a Christian wife."

Nothing had come of it, but at the New Year's party, Richard grabbed Erma by both hands and then looked at me. "Aren't you ashamed of yourself for taking this gorgeous creature out of circulation?" He laughed as he spoke, and Erma seemed to share his gaiety.

Disgusting, I thought, and I withdrew into the dining room where I sat sulking, drinking a little of the harmless punch and sampling the cake. The evening was a social failure for me, although Erma was having a ball, especially when she was laughing with Richard King.

On the way home, Erma unknowingly added fuel to my smoldering jealousy. "Sherry, why didn't you ever introduce me to Richard back last summer, before we were married? You know Charlotte thought he would be just the right man for me."

Erma's voice was light and gay. She did not seem to notice that I had pulled my heavy coat around my skinny body and was trying to shrink down into the crack of the seat. Her tinkling voice chattered on.

"I can remember, too, when Mildred Day told me that she thought *you* would be the right one for me."

"She did?" I mumbled. "What did you tell her?"

"I said, 'Mildred Day, you're no friend of mine!' And I really meant it. I certainly never thought it would work out the way it has."

Yeah, I thought. *And look how it has worked out.*

I put a second log on the dying fire, then a third. Squirming around on the bench, I tried to find a position where the heat could hit my back and ease the pain. What a miserable life this was.

Christmas, I recalled, had been such a disappointment. No one wanted to go to a midnight service, and I had never known Christmas without one. And the bills. I shuddered to think of what the mail would bring over the next several weeks. Then there was Margie. Her whole future loomed before me. One thing was certain, she could not live here with this new family of mine. We had tried it over Christmas, and it had been a near disaster.

And as always, lurking in the background was my impotence. After my talk with Earle, I had hoped things would be better. But somehow our times of lovemaking had turned into our times of bitterest arguments. Once Erma had told me, "I can't stand to see you lying beside me, leering at me. Your face looks like a demon."

Well, that kind of conversation has a way of taking all the starch out of lovemaking. It took us half the night to stop shouting at each other so we could finally get to sleep—in separate rooms.

Margie's being with us for Christmas had not helped matters either. There were many things about the household she didn't like, and more than once she spoke her thoughts quite tactlessly. Her critical remarks to the children, which were received in sullen silence, built the tension to the boiling point. And her remarks to Erma—the "oh-daddy-and-I-don't-do-things-like-that" kind of remarks—heated the fire so the pressure in the house was at the stage of explosion.

I groaned. "Why, oh why, can't she control her tongue?" Then the answer came—straight from the pit. "Like father, like son—only this time it's like daughter." I found myself once again agreeing with Satan's logic. How right he was. I knew that my own tongue was my weakest point. Almost every quarrel Erma and I had experienced up to that moment could have been prevented if I had only kept silent a little longer.

"You always have to have the last word," Erma had a way of saying. And I invariably fell into the trap of saying something else to explain why I had to say whatever it was that I had just said. I did have to have the last word. After all, wasn't I always right?

In any case, I knew for certain that it would not do to try to fit my daughter into this little house. But how could we afford a bigger one, heavily in debt as we were—and with those lots up in the Poconos still to be paid for? And now the county taxes were coming due.

Erma and I had several fruitless discussions as to how we could solve these and many other problems. We finally agreed that only God could solve them. Erma's idea, however, was that God would do it by bringing us help from the outside, whereas I contended He would aid us only if we made more of an effort to work out the solution for ourselves. We could learn to be more economical; we could arrange our time more efficiently. We could start by hewing

away at the huge mountain of clutter in Erma's house which
had accumulated over twenty-three years. Much of it should
be thrown away, I contended.

"God helps those who help themselves," I quoted piously.

"Where do you find that in the Bible?" she asked.

I had to confess that it wasn't Scripture at all, just plain
common sense. Even the Bible became something to quarrel
about. We came at it from exactly opposite points of view.
Erma knew very little of what was actually in the Book, but
asserted almost fiercely that she believed every word in it.
After having been a minister for fifty-six years, I knew it fairly
well, but because I had been trained back in seminary days to
explain away a great deal of the supernatural part of it, it
seemed to Erma I was actually defending heresy. The fact
that I had renounced my modernism and really believed the
Bible to be God's Word, the fact that I had received the
Baptism in the Holy Spirit and was actually experiencing
miracles in my ministry, did not keep Erma from arguing
with me—often on minor points of interpretation. And
because I always insisted on the last word, and because she
always had to make one final rebuttal following my last word,
our arguments went on and on like the *Gloria Patri*—world
without end.

We had, in short, found that almost anything we talked
about led us into an argument. We had a way of making up
before we went to sleep, but even the making up often led to
arguments. One night we kissed and then prayed, "We'll try
harder, dear Lord, we'll try harder next time." Then I added,
"Please, oh please, help me guard my tongue."

"Amen!" Erma said firmly.

"What did you mean by that?" I said caustically.

"I was saying 'Amen' to your prayer that you needed to

have your tongue guarded. And obviously that prayer has not yet been answered." Off we went into a shouting match, necessitating another kiss-and-make-up and more prayer. It seemed we were getting worse, rather than better—becoming more like two people rather than drawing closer together as one.

I stirred the fire in front of me and added two more logs. It was really blazing now. I sat back, wincing at the pain in my back. Why did I tackle that tree so hard when I just wasn't used to work of that kind? Was it really out of temper? Lord, if I'd only not had to have that last word.

I had flared up again about the bills. "You didn't use even half of those things you bought on our honeymoon to give as Christmas presents, like you said you were going to," I complained. "They are still packed away in the attic in those old suitcases."

"Honeymoon!" Erma had countered. "Do you call what we had a honeymoon? We were never alone after the first night, and even that night wasn't much. Besides, you were always so worried about money, money, money. It's your God. It's all you ever think about. And you didn't bring me into a new house like you brought your second wife. With Thelma everything was new. But Erma gets the leftovers."

"That's enough, *Therma*," I shouted, stuttering in my anger.

"*Therma!* So, that's who I am now. Half Thelma and half Erma. No wonder the kids think you are a phony. You don't love them, you don't love us. All you love is yourself—and Margie."

"I don't!" I shouted. "I worry about *you*, all the time."

"Why don't you make love to me then, like a real husband? You keep making promises that everything will be

different soon, but you don't keep them. And you gripe
about every cent I spend. How about you? Every time you go
into a store you buy yourself candy. Always for yourself. And
what about that box of candy you said you bought for me at
Christmas? You ate it! Pig! You never have learned to think
of other people. You're *such* a phony!"

"Why didn't you marry a man like King?" I shouted.
There, I had said it. "He's young enough, and rich enough,
to really satisfy your needs."

Erma blazed. We were both shouting now, eager to hurt
each other. We had quite forgotten the children were in the
house. There was more, and afterward I sulked for hours
thinking of the monstrous unfairness of it all. She was so
illogical! How could I have known back in those days with
Thelma that I'd someday be needing money for a third wife
who spent money like it was going out of season? Sure, I had
lavished money from that inheritance on Thelma, and
bought the new house in Florida for her wedding present.
But what did Erma expect me to do now? I was adding my
whole income to hers, and it still wasn't adequate for her
extravagances. And why did she refuse to face the fact that
we now had much less income than we had thought we
would have? My sexual inadequacy faded into comparative
insignificance in my mind at that moment in comparison
with our need for economy—a word that totally escaped
Erma's vocabulary.

The bickering started again after breakfast, after the kids
had gone off to their schools. I asked why last night's supper
dishes were all over the place, food needlessly drying on them
when they could have been so easily rinsed and put in the
dishwasher the way Margie had always done it back in the
apartment.

Erma exploded, and I stormed out the door into the backyard. I looked at the old tree that David had been cutting up for firewood. The saw lay where he had dropped it. No one ever put anything away around here. I grabbed it and began sawing with all my might. This was better than having to shout at Erma.

Then the stab of pain hit my back. Years before, I had fallen on a slippery sidewalk, and my back had bothered me off and on ever since. But this time, I must have really pulled something loose. I dropped the saw, groaning loudly, and staggered back into the house.

If I had expected Erma to feel sorry for me, I was doomed to disappointment. Her reaction was plain disgust. "You know you only went out there and worked so furiously because you were mad at me. You're just a spoiled little boy."

I denied it. I told her I knew David needed some help with that old tree, and since I didn't have anything else to do, I was going to save him some time.

"Sherry, you can't even tell the truth. Not only are you an impotent old skinflint, you're also a liar. Now you've hurt your back, and the rest of us are going to have to suffer because of it. You never stop to think. You're *so* inconsiderate."

I was in no condition for another quarrel. Holding my tongue, I limped off to the bedroom to lie down. In a few minutes, Erma was at my side with an electric hot pad which she had somehow found in the jumbled bathroom closet. She was all sweetness now, the Erma I truly loved.

"Oh Sherry, I am sorry about your back. Lie on this pad. It'll be better soon. Trust Jesus to heal you. Luvaluia, my husband."

I hugged her closely as she fitted the pad under my back. But by evening we were shouting at each other again. Nothing had changed.

I stirred the fire and yawned. It was 5:00 A.M. I needed to get back to bed and try once more to get some sleep. But suddenly I heard an angry voice in the doorway of the living room. Erma stood in the hall. Robert, sleepily rubbing his eyes, was behind her.

"What on earth are you doing out here, Sherry?" Erma scolded. "Robert couldn't sleep. He smelled something hot and came and waked me. Here you've got this fire roaring, and Robert and Dave's room is like an oven. Sherry, what is the matter with you? Can't you ever think of other people and what they need? Must you always think of yourself only?"

I mumbled something about my back . . . the too soft bed . . . the cold room . . . My excuses sounded as lame to me as I knew they must to Erma and Robert, who now slipped off to his own bed. Why, oh why had I been so inconsiderate? Wouldn't I ever learn? Completely frustrated, I permitted Erma to lead me back to bed. Once we were there, her mood changed.

"Sherry, promise me you'll do something about that back today. Maybe you should go see the osteopath who helped David last year when he hurt his back playing football." I promised, and we hugged each other. Thank God, love was still there.

"Count it all joy, Sherry," Erma whispered. "Luvaluia."

Desire flowed back into me, the first I had felt in days and days. And there I was with a back that felt broken and could hardly move, much less make love.

But there was something else present in the bed that morning. Not only love, but hope. Faint, but so sweet. I hugged it tightly. Erma was close beside me. Touching her, I could again touch God.

11
Flat on My Face

It had been almost ten months since I had received that letter from Bill Keller, the president of the Laurel, Mississippi, chapter of the Full Gospel Business Men's Fellowship. I was invited to be one of the speakers at the Regional Conference, the first for the whole Mississippi area. Since it was my first opportunity to speak in one of these big interdenominational conferences, I was excited. The other speakers were all well-recognized national figures —Charles Simpson from Alabama, Kenneth Hagin from Oklahoma, and Ken Sumrall from Florida. Surely when Erma saw me listed on the program with all those dignitaries, and when she heard me stand up and deliver the Word of God while they all sat and listened, she would finally recognize me as a spiritual giant.

My overwhelming eagerness by now was to prove to my wife—and to myself—that I was really somebody of importance in the charismatic movement. Although I knew Erma never considered me "first team" material, this time I was associating with the major leaguers, which was bound to make some kind of impression on her.

We planned our trip so we could stop in several different cities along the way to visit friends, taking advantage of Bill Keller's generous offer to pay all our expenses coming and going. One of the places we wanted to stop was in Johnson City, Tennessee, to see our old friends, Tom and Margaret Happel. Tom, a wealthy business executive, and a fellow Episcopalian was confined to a wheelchair with a growing tumor. Knowing that Kenneth Hagin would be conducting a daily healing seminar at the convention, I hoped we could persuade Tom to attend. Perhaps he would be healed.

We were planning to leave early in order to get to Jackson two days before the convention began. Bill Keller wanted me to appear on local television and hold some interviews with reporters. It was just beginnning to dawn on me that I was not minor-league stuff anymore, I was a major-league star—a Very Important Person.

Tom Happel was in bed when we arrived in Johnson City. However, Margaret assured us he was often up for hours at a time. I had sent them some of Kenneth Hagin's booklets on healing, and they were excited about the possibility of meeting him in Jackson. They would be going in Tom's private plane, with their chauffeur doubling as pilot, and would stop over in Jackson on their way to an important directors' meeting in Texas. Tom had his doctor's assurance that the trip would not be too damaging to his health. I was enthusiastic. Surely this was God's answer to all our prayers for Tom's healing. I knew I could persuade Kenneth Hagin to come up to their room in the convention hotel to pray for Tom. I then prayed for him myself and was gratified by his smile. "I do feel better. Thank you, Rector."

It was Friday night, the night of the big opportunity. I sat there on the platform with about a dozen others, waiting my time to speak. It had been a wonderful week. Tom and Margaret were in the hotel. They should be entering the meeting at any moment.

I was happy at the memory of my first TV appearance. And Erma had assured me I had not been nervous. Indeed, I felt I had really been master of the situation. The TV director had tried to get me to weaken my message. I had refused to take his lead, however, and as a result, the whole city of Jackson knew there was at least one Episcopal priest who spoke in tongues. Bill Keller had congratulated me also, on the strong newspaper article that had appeared that morning in the Jackson *Express*, the city's leading newspaper. Even the elevator boy had greeted me, "Saw you on television this morning." So much publicity was a heady draft. I was not used to it, but I loved it just the same.

I looked out at the great sea of faces before me, an ocean of people waiting to hear me speak. I trusted the warm glow inside me was the Holy Spirit, yet, I had a tiny twinge of conscience. I wished I had not taken that drink of whiskey before coming to the platform.

It had happened upstairs in Tom Happel's room. Kenneth Hagin had graciously consented to accompany me to the Happels' room and talk with them after the afternoon service. He prayed for Tom, and I fully expected him to leap from his wheelchair and dance around the room. But nothing happened.

After Hagin left the room, Margaret called room service and had cocktails sent up. I had an uneasy feeling. I should return to my own room in the hotel and pray before the meeting, but I hated to leave the Happels. Erma, of course, was going to stay with them, but what about me? I wavered, then said I'd stay.

I remembered the last time I had been with the Happels. It was up in their mountain cottage, and they had served me whiskey, saying that every Episcopal priest they knew was able to "hold his likker." They didn't know I was one of the exceptions, and soon after taking my drink of bourbon, I had gone sound asleep in their living room, right in the middle of a conversation. Erma was mortified.

Now they had ordered me a whiskey sour, just minutes before I was to be the main speaker of the evening to the regional gathering of charismatics. I took the drink and choked it down—much to their merriment—and then excused myself to come down to the meeting room and take my place on the platform. Thank God, though, the whiskey did not seem to be making me sleepy. Instead I was "'raring to go."

The testimonies of various businessmen were ended, and someone was talking about the offering. My head was a little fuzzy, and I was having trouble focusing my eyes, but I chalked it up to a combination of excitement and old age. Again I had that feeling, "Why is the man taking the offering so long-winded? Doesn't he know all these people have come to hear me?"

Then I was introduced. Mercifully, the introduction was short. But as I stood to speak, I had a frantic feeling. I was all alone. The Holy Spirit, on whom I had counted to speak through me, was nowhere to be found.

Fortunately, or should I say unfortunately, what I lacked in anointing I was able to make up for by verbal eloquence— and long-windedness. I was conscious of keeping my voice under control and making sure it was heard in every corner of

the room. I deliberately planned my gestures, nodded wisely
as I spoke, and kept good eye contact with the audience.
And, thanks to the whiskey which seemed to have liberally
loosened my tongue, I had no difficulty in telling my story.
Although I had told the same story many times, this time it
seemed I had a new command of the English language, using
words I had never used before, and telling the story with a
great wealth of detail—and in great length. Great length.

I noticed that Erma and the Happels had entered the
room. The little commotion at the back, caused when people
made room for the wheelchair, distracted me from where I
was in my story. But I soon got started again, although I had
the strange feeling that I was retelling great portions that I
had already told earlier in the hour.

I went on talking—forty, fifty, sixty more minutes. I tried
hard to make up for the lack of inspiration of the Holy Spirit
by being more rhetorical than ever. I must place my voice
just right. I spoke now softly, now louder. But it was all
mechanical, without a shred of inspiration or anointing. My
testimony was all true—how could it come out of my lips
sounding so unreal, so unconvincing even to my own ears? I
continued to talk, thinking that quantity would make up for
quality. I could not seem to stop. A dozen times I must have
said, "Now, in conclusion," and used the phrase as a
springboard to launch into some other irrelevant tale. I
hardly know, even now, how I finally brought it to an end.

All I could think of, as I sank into my seat, was, "I've
muffed it." And I was so sure that my talk would inspire
people. Yet I had rambled on for nearly two hours and said
absolutely nothing. All I could see before my eyes were those
bored looks and people squirming in their chairs. "Oh God,

why do I bungle things so? Why didn't I take time for prayer, like I did before the television show? Why did I have to try and impress the Happels that I was a good fellow by drinking even a sip of that whiskey sour?"

I looked around and saw that the room was almost empty now. No one had come up to talk to me. They had streamed forward when the other speakers had finished. I had imagined how I would be mobbed and thronged. Instead, I was ignored as the people quickly made their way out of the room. That was fine with me. I didn't want to talk to a soul. Poor Bill Keller. How I had let him down.

I hurried to the back of the room just in time to grab Tom's hand as he was being wheeled out. "Can't you possibly stay over for the meeting tomorrow?" I asked him. "You know, Kenneth Hagin says the power flows so much more strongly when there are many believers together."

But Tom assured me it was impossible, and Margaret said, "I must get him back to his room now. We leave pretty early. We really cannot miss that directors' meeting—Tom is chairman of the board. After all," she said glancing at her watch, "it is pretty late."

I stumbled back down the aisle. Erma had disappeared, and the whiskey was beginning to work its old tricks as I yawned and supported myself on the chairs as I walked. The room was really empty now. But what was it Bill had said about the prayer room for those who needed ministry? Yes, that's where I should be. Maybe I could make up for my failure by ministering to those in need.

I pushed my way into the little room. A score of men and women were sitting around the walls. An earnest young minister whom I did not recognize was addressing them. All eyes were intent upon him. Without waiting for him to finish, I blurted out, "I'm here now. I've come to pray for any of you that want prayer."

I glanced around and saw Erma standing in the corner of the room, her face white with anguish as she made strange motions with her hands. Ignoring her signals, I blundered on. "My wife is here also. That's her over there in the corner. She can pray for you, too."

Two hours later, we were back in our bedroom. Erma had not said a single word—as we walked to the elevator, as we got off on the tenth floor, as we put the key in the lock. How I longed to hear some expression of approval. My talk had undoubtedly been dry and much too long, but at least she should be proud of me for my bold ministry in the prayer room.

We undressed in silence, and I finally spoke, desperate to receive her approval. "Did you know that the young man who received that wonderful deliverance in the prayer room was the son of the Baptist minister we met in Florida?"

Erma's voice was icy. "Yes, I heard him say so." Ignoring me, she crept into bed and started to pull the covers up around her face.

I pleaded with her now, almost frightened. "Erma, I know I fell down badly tonight. I had you and the Happels too much on my mind." I put my hand out to touch her, to draw her to me as I sat on the side of the bed.

"It wasn't just that!" she spit out, turning over with her eyes blazing. "Oh, I could almost hate you, you blithering old idiot. Don't even touch me. How could you embarrass me so? 'My wife can pray, too!' You blundered into the prayer room like a drunken jackass, interrupting without the slightest consideration for that young minister. He was really ministering life to those people. If you had just listened instead of trying to show off. Oh, Sherry, you have less discernment than anyone else I have ever known."

I rose slowly to my feet and stood facing the mirror over the cluttered dresser, filled with Erma's creams, booklets and a little of everything else. I saw myself for who I was. A skinny old priest who should have been dead forty years ago, still stumbling around the world getting in people's way.

Then I saw things from Erma's point of view. And I saw that God had been truly merciful to this old priest. Had I made an outward success of my talk after having made so little effort to seek God's anointing, I would have felt I could just go on and on in my own strength. Instead, He had allowed me to fall flat on my face in the hour of my greatest opportunity, teaching me that without Him I was just Bill Sherwood. And Bill Sherwood—without Jesus—was nothing but a bumbling old fool.

The next morning at the close of the service we were standing around the base of the platform. I glanced up and saw an old man in his seventies bounding up to Erma and me. He seemed to be half drunk, but it was not "spirits" this time, it was the Holy Spirit that was making him so deliriously happy. He said he had driven halfway home the night before when he realized he had been healed from lifelong asthma. Turning his car around, he had driven back eighty miles just to testify this morning of what had happened to him. He embraced me so hard I almost collapsed under his hug. "And you're the old minister who prayed for me last night!" he shouted.

What a wonderful, loving, forgiving God we have. What

power He has to use even the most unworthy tools. For once I felt more humble than elated as I recalled the time in the prayer room the night before. I looked around at Erma. She was beaming. This time God Himself had let her approve of me. Perhaps, just perhaps, God was not through with me yet.

12

Satisfaction in the Sun

Erma was busy looking over her wardrobe, part of which was hanging in Nancy's closet, part in John's, and part stuffed in a closet at the end of the hall. John had married during the spring, and he and his wife were living in another part of the city. This gave Erma and me a bedroom, even if it did have twin beds. Margie had made the big decision—thanks to Archer Torrey's recommendation—to become a secretary in a newly formed charismatic community at Scottsdale, Arizona. After two years of happy service there, she would settle with her brother and sister-in-law in Rochester, New York. We were gradually becoming a more orderly family, even if Erma still hung her clothes all over the house.

"School's out this weekend, and we're all going camping down near Myrtle Beach," she informed me. "Nancy and I are going shopping this afternoon for some camp clothes. Let's see, Sherry, you'll need two pairs of levis, and we'll cut the legs off one pair at the knees. You won't need a windbreaker—this one of John's will do fine, and—"

"But I've got plenty of old clothes good enough for camp," I protested.

"Sherry, you don't want to look like an old man, do you? Those things of yours—we'll send them to the Salvation Army. The kids want you to look sharp."

I decided the cost of new levis was not enough to justify a longer argument, but I couldn't resist asking, "Erma, why are you always so interested in dressing us up in new clothes?"

"When I was a little girl," she laughed, "my mother was always dressing me up like a doll. Now, I guess, I like to dress people up like she did me."

A deeper thought had struck me which I did not venture to express. Why had she not consulted me before promising the children we would go camping? I was supposed to be the head of this house, the one to make the decisions. How did she know I hadn't some plans myself? True, Erma had more than once told me she loved camping, and she knew I loved it too. But it bothered me that if the kids really wanted to do something, she always gave in—without asking me.

I didn't want to start another argument with Erma, and soon I was throwing myself into the project with as great enthusiasm as the children. Nancy would take Mary Lou, the girl who lived next door, and David would take his best friends, Jimmy Harper and Rick Bacot who was also Nancy's boyfriend. Robert, still having classes at the university, would drive down on the weekends.

One thing soon became clear: the project was good for the kids. They jockeyed the camper from its position in the driveway, where it had stood through the winter with its sprung hasp, and pulled it out onto the front lawn. There they swept and scrubbed, filled water and gas tanks, and replaced the cooking dishes and other items that belonged in the cabinets. Robert kept reminding us we must start long before daylight Monday morning. He would take two days off from school to help us pitch camp.

"The big thing is to get there ahead of the crowd," he warned. "That's the only way you'll get a site close to the ocean."

"How long do you expect we'll stay?" I asked Erma, the whole thing being out of my hands anyway.

"Over the Fourth of July," she beamed. "That's when Robert gets a long weekend. Anyway, that's the day the kids are looking forward to. They say we mustn't miss it at the beach."

Again I felt that obscure uneasiness at the thought. A Christian family, it seemed, should have a father at the head. Not three children. However, they were apparently making all the decisions.

One happy thought did occur which I followed through on. I called my son Bob in Raleigh and suggested he, his wife and three children should bring their tent and join us.

It was midmorning, very bright and very hot, when we finally reached the camping ground and made out an application for a campsite.

"Pick out any unoccupied site and let us know the number," the attendant said.

The boys had canvassed the possibilities as near as possible to the seashore, only to find no sites left in the row that faced the ocean. They were disappointed, but they were quickly comforted when we found a lot only a couple of hundred yards back from the front rank. They sprang out of the car to stake their claim, unhitched the camper, and eased it into position. I could not get over my amazement as I watched the dexterity with which they raised the top, opened it up, fastened on the canvas sides, and got the curtains into place. There was also a tent to be pitched to one side where the sleeping bags, spare blankets, and extra equipment could be stored. I had thought the children might sleep in the tent so Erma and I could have the camper. However, they quickly informed me that snakes might come into the tent, so they would share the camper with us.

Erma said the camper itself could sleep eight persons. She and I were to share the bed at one end, Nancy and her friend the one at the opposite end, and in-between, beds could be pulled into position at night for David, Jimmy and Rick. Robert would just have to take his chances with the snakes.

Erma and I were excited. We would have a regular bed at last, a bed far nicer than the twin beds we had to crowd into in John's room. We stretched out side by side to try it. "You can unbuckle the side curtains at night and look out at the stars," she told me. Our only separation from the others in the camper would be a thin curtain, but at least it was opaque. Memories of Pullman car trips in the old days danced in my mind. I always did love to travel in a sleeping car. I could hardly wait for night to come.

"No time to make love now," she laughed at me. "We have work to do."

I sat out in the dazzling sun and watched the boys, fascinated by their quick young efficiency. I was feeling suddenly very old, utterly weak—but I realized it was only one of "those attacks" that was robbing me of my energy. I'd had them before and learned to live with them—probably some defect in my blood sugar. I was satisfied to sit still and let it pass over. I felt like such a fifth wheel, anyway. Always in the past, I had been the one on our family camping trips to boss the job. Now I had to sit out in the sun like an old dog, energyless and mooning, while the kids worked so hard.

Erma was shaking me. "Sherry! Stop looking so old!"

I pulled myself together with an effort. "It's only one of those spells," I protested. "I've told you about them before."

But she was pitiless. "I notice you always get those attacks when you don't get your own way. Now forget it and enjoy the camp."

She handed me a coil of nylon rope and said, "You'll feel better if you help the boys. Here, put up a clothesline for the towels and blankets, and stake out the poles for the front tarpaulin."

I could have slapped her if I hadn't felt so tired. But her casual treatment of my "weak spell" was just the tonic I needed. I felt better as soon as I got busy with the rope, cutting off the unneeded portion and putting it back in the storage space under the bed.

It was good to be camping once more. The beautiful white sand, the foamy breakers, and the blue, blue stretch of sea brought a serenity I had not felt for years. The knee-length levis Nancy had prepared for me were very comfortable, and they made me feel at home in the company of the young people, who were everywhere. My beard, too, which I had let grow at Erma's suggestion after our return from Jackson, really seemed to let me fit in with the teenage boys David ran around with. It made me less, rather than more, conspicuous. The only problem arose when I rounded the corner of the camper one day and came face to face with a little boy in a bathing suit. He took one look at me, dropped his sand bucket, and ran screaming to his father.

"Daddy, who is that man? I don't like him," he bawled.

His father pressed him against his wet, hairy chest and told me apologetically, "Don't mind him. He's always been afraid of Santa Claus."

I rubbed my white whiskers thoughtfully. Maybe I had better shave after all. Yet Erma's story of having had a vision of making love to a man with a snowy white beard convinced me I should keep it on. Who could tell? That day might arrive even yet.

It didn't take me long to adapt to the lazy, relaxing rhythm of beach life. To be sure, I was worried about the expense involved in our being here so long. Nearly everything, including the rental of the seldom-used beach umbrella, cost money. Yet there were some things that were free which compensated for the rest. The little crabs that peeked out so cautiously and then darted out across the sand, the wheeling gulls that lighted near us, the birds on a piling of a pier, or the sight of a distant ship on the blue horizon—all seemed adequate repayment for the money spent. Perhaps I was loosening up and trusting God to supply our needs after all. It felt good.

Sleeping together in one bed, too, during those lovely starlit nights, had special compensation. Watching the moon start its nightly journey through its phases, bigger each night as we looked out through the side curtains, had its healing and its quiet joy. The God of nature was very close.

But the experience of being so close to Erma was also tantalizing. We longed to make love, but were conscious, of course, of the two girls at the far end of the camper and the boys almost at our feet. There just was no opportunity.

"We'll just have to forget all that while we are here," Erma whispered in my ear. "Besides, you didn't bring any of those pills the Pineville doctor gave you to stimulate your drive. I haven't seen you taking them for weeks."

She was right. I had gone to see a doctor who specialized in such problems. He had loaded me down with more than two hundred dollars' worth of pills. Not only had they not improved my sex drive one bit, but I was staying awake at night worrying how I was going to pay the pharmacy bill.

The worst thing about those pills were the instructions. I was to take them six hours before intercourse. And how could I know whether other factors would make any particular night a time to engage in marital love? For one thing, it was distasteful to Erma to have me ask at 3:00 P.M. whether she felt like trying again that night. She much preferred to be "turned on" by something romantic, rather than by six hours prior notice by an old man standing in the bathroom with a bottle of potency pills in his hand.

Actually our sex life—or should I say our striving to have a sex life—had become less important to us as the months wore on. John's wedding on Easter Day had consumed our interest. Then there was a trip to Florida where I consulted with a Spirit-filled physician, Dr. Bill Reed, who told me I needed to stop trying so hard and just act natural. While in Florida, we had visited with our friend, dear Joanna Wood. Not only had she loaned us money to help us out of our financial bind, but had strongly advised Erma to get out of the land deal in the Poconos. We had heeded her advice, much to my relief.

Then there had been a trip to the Tennessee-Georgia Christian camp and a talk with Derek Prince. When I had told him of my marital problems and how I had actually contemplated divorce, he had said sternly, "There are some rooms which a man should lock and throw away the key." In other words, there could be no way *out* of a bad or uncomfortable marriage, only *up* and *through*. His strong direction in telling me God did not will us to divorce helped me shut that door. Now I was busy trying to throw away the key.

Yet it had been through Archer and Jane Torrey that I had gained my deepest insight. The Torreys had found an apartment close by us while Archer was serving as curate at Christ Church before they returned to their mission in Korea. More than once when Archer was out of town, Erma and I would spend the night in their apartment—a welcome break in our routine. Jane's quiet prayer life, her easy sharing and utter lack of pretentiousness were soothing. Away from our own crowded home, Erma and I came much nearer a honeymoon love life than we could in our own bedroom. Probably the greatest factor in this was the quiet prayer time with Jane. We no longer felt like phonies, as we did much of the time at home. God was nearer and more real, and that, in turn, allowed us to feel more forgiving of one another. We were learning that the presence of God was more important than any aphrodisiac.

Gradually I began to realize that only God had the real answer to my impotence. And without trying, I began to allow Him full access into every detail of my sex life. We discovered that when we knew Jesus was present, blessing our every word and action, covering us with His love, energizing our love, that what had been a chore could become a dazzlingly beautiful love encounter that would light up our whole lives.

Early one afternoon, as we lay side by side on the sand, the hot sun beating against our bodies and the rented umbrella,

as usual, wasting its shade a few feet from us, we took each
other by the hand and rolled over, facing each other. We
both felt it, like an electric current between us. Strong,
almost like an animal desire. I was momentarily afraid. All
my life I had been taught that sexual love should be
"spiritual." Yet what I was now feeling for Erma was a
different kind of love. Erotic. Sensual. Could this, too, be of
God?

"Let's go back to the camper and see where everyone is."
I'm not even sure which one of us said the words, we each
knew so well what was in the other's thoughts. And we
walked to the camper hand in hand.

We saw the camps all around us completely deserted; they
would be, this time of day. We opened the door and bolted
it behind us, and without a word we made love in a hungry,
deep, almost animal way. We did not pray. We did not ask
God to bless our lovemaking. We just went at each other as
healthy animals come instinctively to the mating encounter.

The sensations were deeply gratifying. For the first time,
both of us exploded in a climactic surge of passion. From the
physical point of view, it was the most thoroughly satisfying
love encounter we had ever had together. The fact that it was
an *eros* type of love, rather than the *agape* type which I had
been continually striving for, bothered me. Deep inside, I
began to understand that we were to glorify God in our
bodies as well as in our spirits. He had let us come together,
finally, on a physical level. Now when our spirits could be
joined also, we would experience a type of love most couples
know nothing about.

We lay side by side on the camper bed. Perfectly relieved.
The sensations completely gone, and the intense pleasure of
our passion quickly only a memory. We returned to the

beach, still hand in hand, hardly saying a word. We never talked of it again. And the very next night, we had one of the first quarrels we had had in weeks.

I don't even remember what it was about, but I remember how we both sulked. Erma had gone on to bed, turning her back toward me. I couldn't sleep. It was intolerable to lie beside her and not hold her. In spite of the experience the afternoon before, we were unchanged in our spirits. I couldn't stand it.

Creeping out of bed, I stepped over the sleeping boys with infinite caution in every movement. The little door of the camper creaked, but no one stirred. In the dark, I dug my own sleeping bag out of the confused pile of bags and spare blankets in the otherwise empty tent behind the camper, and made my way, with a triumphant feeling, to the deserted seashore. The waves, splashing so quietly and edged with white in the moonlight, were my only companions. I spread the sleeping bag safely above the high-water mark, close to the marsh grass. Here, I thought, a man can really pray! I lay back gazing up at the night sky, and feeling the caress of the night breeze on my face. My last waking thoughts were of Erma. I hoped she would awake, find me gone, wonder where I was, and feel sorry that she had driven me out of my bed.

Suddenly I felt my bedroll shaking. The moon was much lower than it had been when I lay down. An angry voice was saying, almost in my ear, "So, here is where you've run away to. Don't you know there are snakes in the marsh grass? Haven't you the slightest consideration for me and what it all must seem like to the kids when you sneak out like this? Oh Sherry, I thought you really were my husband at last, but you're only a spoiled child."

Suddenly ashamed of myself, I gathered my sleeping things together and meekly followed my wife back to the camper where I climbed carefully back into the bed beside her. I had succeeded, somewhat. She had missed me all right, but it was not turning out the way I had expected.

"We've not been praying together much since we came to camp," I whispered. "Yesterday afternoon was wonderful, but there's got to be more or we'll be back where we started. Oh Lord Jesus, help me to stop making such a mess of things."

Erma was praying softly also. We kissed, embraced, and fell asleep.

It was after midnight the next night when Erma and I returned to the camp. We had been visiting friends in nearby Myrtle Beach and during an impromptu after-dinner prayer meeting, one of them had received the Baptism in the Holy Spirit. Erma and I couldn't keep from singing with joy as we drove the twelve miles back to the campsite. Her hand was in mine as back in the old days of our trips before our marriage.

"How quickly He forgives our sins," she said softly. I squeezed her hand. We were completely in tune that minute, for those very thoughts had been in my own heart. We sang even louder.

The watchman was at the gate. He had evidently heard us coming. He looked a bit suspicious and seemed to be trying to get close enough to smell our breath.

"We've just come from a prayer meeting," Erma said as I sat beside her, still singing.

"Uh huh," he muttered, flashing his light over in my eyes. I admit we must have looked like a strange pair. This young woman driving a big car and a skinny little old man with a snow-white beard sitting beside her—singing. However, he let us in, and we made our way through the darkened camp to our camper.

A strange tent was pitched right on the edge of our site, actually overlapping it. Strange clothing was draped over our clothesline. The wall of the new tent was almost touching the end of our camper. This would never do.

The song in our hearts dragged to a stop. We looked at each other. "Shall we wake them and tell them they don't belong so close to us?" Erma asked. "They're just squatting on our site."

We decided to drive back to the gate and inform the night watchman of the problem. Our hearts were too full of joy to cause trouble for anyone, but we did want to advise the authorities.

The watchman heard our story and called the other night watchman in the prowl car by walkie-talkie. By the time we had returned to our camper, the prowl car had arrived, and there, in the combined moonlight and the glare of the headlights, stood a tall, sleepy young man in his pajamas.

"This man says he is expected," the night watchman said. "Is he?"

"Dad! Don't you recognize your own son? I'm Bob."

I had forgotten. I had invited him down from Raleigh and now I was about to have him arrested.

He had found our camper and put up his tent, just as we had told him to do. I was glad that the lights playing on the scene weren't bright enough to show how red my face was under my beard. We finally got everybody settled down, and I went to sleep in Erma's arms, thinking how good it was to have my own son next door.

Robert was with us for the weekend, making himself

useful. The tarpaulin was flapping too hard in the rising wind, and he looked for rope, finding the piece I'd cut off from the nylon coil the first day.

"Hey, who cut this good rope?" he complained.

Erma saw it for the first time. "Sherry! Why did you have to cut it? Now you have ruined it for us to use at home." And the argument began. No use pointing out I knew a Boy Scout knot that would make it as good as new. In my heart, I knew it wouldn't. And of course the real trouble was the old one. I hated to fall down in the eyes of Erma and her son as a bungler—and didn't know how to assert myself without making matters worse.

This time help came from another corner. David and Nancy came flying to my rescue. "Hey, lay off Sherry. He's our friend and was only trying to help. You'd never use that rope at home anyway."

Erma backed off, not used to hearing her children take my side. Maybe progress was being made after all.

The Fourth came all too soon, and we broke camp for home. Safely back in Charlotte with the camper parked on the front lawn, Erma and I turned to one another with one thought.

"Let's sleep out here," she said. We both laughed. The camper bed was pretty special, and far more roomy than the single beds in John's room. So, for the rest of the summer and into the fall, we did our loving in the camper—where it had all begun. What if it did mean risking the neighbors' surprised looks when they saw us emerge in the morning and race each other across the wet grass for the house. This was our home away from everyone. It got started here. It would continue here. And here we could really let our love be free.

It was here in the camper that another of our prayers was answered. I awakened before dawn on the first day of October to hear the sound of what I thought was the singing of many birds—or angels. It was Erma, lying beside me, singing in high clear tones words I could not understand. At last she had received her gift of tongues—the gift she had prayed for ever since she had received her Baptism in the Holy Spirit accompanied by the holy laughter. She prayed and sang alternately that morning for at least two hours, never loud, and almost unable to stop. What an important part this was to play in our lives in the months to come as we came closer and closer together in the spirit—praying and singing and rejoicing together. How fitting, that here in the camper where we first truly became one flesh, we should also come together in the Spirit.

13

Continuing Discoveries

Two and a half years had passed, and our love life was no longer a problem, though it was not by any means the important thing we had thought it would be during those early days of our marriage. I was now eighty-two, and sex had begun to take its rightful place. There were many times of deep excitement when we came together in physical love. Realizing that God was God of *eros* love as well as of *agape* love had set me free. I had always believed that anything sensual was not of God, that the flesh was meant to be crucified, not enjoyed. Now with the new understanding that God wanted me to glorify Him in my body as well as in my spirit, I had been released from the bondage that had prevented me from loving and satisfying my wife sexually. We were on our way to becoming one flesh.

Part of the insight into God's plan came in an unexpected way. Erma and I were returning to Charlotte after a visit to Florida. We spent the final night with friends in Augusta, Georgia, who graciously put us in their guest room. As always, it was somewhat of a disappointment to me to be shown to a room with twin beds, especially when they were on opposite sides of the room. But we were thoroughly fatigued, and so were soon fast asleep.

Long before daylight, however, I found myself wide-awake and full of desire to be in bed with Erma. I lay there in the semidarkness (our hostess had thoughtfully left a night-light burning in an adjoining room) and tried to put down the strong desire to make love to my wife. Instead, the desire grew stronger. How I hungered for a really close union with her, that we might be one in flesh and soul alike. The thought came to me that I could creep into bed with her, rouse her, urge her, make love to her. After all, didn't I have "marriage rights"? How often I had heard that expression.

I got out of bed quietly and stood over her, watching the faint outline of her body, listening to her slow, deep breathing. At home she would wake at a touch or a sound; the thought of the children in the next rooms always seemed to keep her from completely relaxing. Here though, she slept soundly, peacefully. She looked so sweet to me now that the desire to wake her, caress her, make love to her, grew so strong it was almost irresistible. But something held me back. I knew she was unusually tired, having done all that driving from Florida without help from me. She had a right to sleep. Yet didn't I have a right to make love to this wife of mine? How these "rights" came into conflict!

I stood there, looking at her, my desire still burning in my loins. Yet it just didn't seem right to waken her. She needed to be rested for tomorrow's journey.

Reluctantly, I climbed back into bed and started thinking. What does the Bible say about marriage rights? Once more I arose, stole into the adjoining bathroom, and consulted my pocket Testament. It was Saint Paul's words in I Corinthians 7 that I was seeking.

"Let the husband render unto the wife due benevolence, and likewise also the wife unto the husband" (v.3). I knew the modern versions put the matter quite clearly. "Due benevolence" meant if the one partner was desirous of sexual intercourse, the other was not to refuse. The passage went on, "The wife hath not power of her own body, but the husband; and likewise also the husband hath not power of his own body, but the wife. Defraud ye not one another [don't cheat each other of the relation that makes marriage, marriage] except it be with consent for a time, that ye may give yourselves to fasting and prayer; and come together again, that Satan tempt you not" (v.4,5).

It was plain enough, I thought. A man does have marital rights, and the wife must consent to satisfy him. Yet to insist on one's "rights" seemed so selfish.

I prayed, "Throw the light of Your Spirit upon this passage, Lord. What do You want me to learn?"

The familiar voice in my heart, the one I had come to recognize as that of Jesus, answered clearly.

"You see it now, My little sheep? She whom you have made your wife and whom I gave you to love and cherish, has indeed a right to expect you to make love to her—when she needs it. And you have a 'right' to accede to her desire. In turn, you have a right to have her accept you as her lover when you need it. But your real 'rights' are to lay down your desires, your very lives—each for the other. That is really what My servant Paul says to you.

Erma no longer belongs to herself, and you no longer belong to yourself. As I laid down My life for My church, My bride, so you have the privilege of laying down your life for your bride. If you waked her and made love to her because she needed it more than sleep, I would bless your act greatly. But you know better. You know that you were thinking only of your momentary desire. And already, you see, I have taken care of that. You are truly happy right now because of your sacrifice of personal desire. Thus you have learned to love her better, to love her with My love and not your human love which has so much self-gratification mixed up in it. You surrendered what you have been thinking of as 'your rights' in favor of her right—her right to unbroken rest. She would gladly do the same thing for you. Do you not, at this moment, feel more fulfilled as a man than if you had wakened her for sexual relations? Isn't it better to be one with Me?"

By now I was glowing all over with the joy of the Lord who was making Himself so real to me. How clearly I saw it all now! Erma had no longer a "right" to her own body. Her body was mine, and if I demanded it, she should be willing to yield. But to *demand* it would be to forfeit three valuable things: 1) the privilege of putting her real, present need (at this time, her need for unbroken rest) ahead of my desire; 2) the privilege of having Christ express His desire for Erma's and my best good, in and through me; 3) the joy of loving her sexually only at the moment when she really wanted it.

I was His slave. What rights does a slave have? True, he can expect his master to look out for him, to take care of him, and to use him as the Master chooses. But that is all.

Joy was mounting in my heart as I turned off the light in the bathroom and tiptoed back to bed. Christ had won another victory in me.

Safely in bed, I felt the warm glow of Christ's beautiful

love all over me. Erma was stirring. "Are you awake, Sherry? What time is it? Don't you want to get in bed with me and cuddle up? I'm cold."

"Thank You, Jesus," I whispered as I climbed out of bed and crossed the room again.

It was hard to keep from shouting as I whispered in Erma's ear, our bodies so close together. "Honey, do you know what? I've just made a wonderful discovery. I have no rights. I am Christ's slave."

"That's beautiful," Erma murmured, snuggling her warm body up close against mine. Strange, how the joy of loving contact could, for the time, seem even sweeter than fulfilled sex.

It was dawn now, and we knew our hostess would be calling us in a few minutes. But happiness in one another, and in Him who made us one in the Spirit as well as in the flesh, overflowed our whole beings. Happiness, given us because we had let go of the right to have happiness. There was a closeness that was as beautiful as perfectly fulfilled sexual expression—although we knew that, too, would come again in its good time. His yoke is easy to bear.

Days later, the full implication of what the Holy Spirit had shown me of the meaning of I Corinthians 7 burst upon me. It was to transform my entire sex life, and Erma's too, bringing us far greater happiness in sex relations than we had known before. If "the husband has no power of his own body, but the wife has" (i.e., a married man's body belongs to his wife—not to himself), then even if he does not feel sexual desire at the time his wife does, it will be given him by the Lord—just to fulfill her need. And I found in experience that this was literally true. It was no longer necessary for me to be potent or even sexually aroused when my wife expressed a desire for sexual love. I could trust God to give me what I needed at the exact moment it was needed.

It was just a case of learning to really trust God on the basis of His word. Knowing that I never had to "grasp the moment" for fear it would pass and I'd be left impotent and Erma left unsatisfied, took all the strain out of our relationship. It made it easier for us to do the other thing Saint Paul suggests, to "abstain for a time, that ye may give yourselves to fasting and to prayer." It made it possible for me to be ever so much more self-controlled than before, because of the Lord's whispered reminder—"If this time passes, there will be a better time in the not too distant future." And this knowledge—that God can and will take care of this aspect in the life of a man who surrenders his will to God's will—set me free.

The secret lay in surrendering the sex act to God, as one should surrender every other act of his life, with constant realization of the presence of Christ. Since Erma and I have been given a prayer language, we often use it while we are making love to one another. Bringing Christ right into the most intimate of all relations, asking Him to bless every aspect of it, not only heightens the sexual experience, but sanctifies it to His glory.

Keeping Jesus in the center of our love life has taken away the least thought of impurity or lust and has gradually transferred our *eros* love (which God did not condemn) to His highest type of love, *agape*. Our bedroom has become a sanctuary, our bed an altar of praise.

14

Perfect Submission—
Perfect Delight

Despite the fact that many of our personal problems seemed to be working themselves out under God's direction, we still had some deep spiritual problems that kept presenting themselves. Erma and I were embarking on a new quest. Where were we to find our proper "spiritual covering"? To whom were we to be in submission? Everywhere we had been during our four years of marriage, we kept hearing these words—submission, covering. It was obvious God's people were no longer satisfied to remain on the superficial level of "going to church." They wanted the deeper walk in the Spirit. And at last, Erma and I were ready for it also.

From what we read in the Bible and heard from our spiritual teachers, it seemed that for our home to come into divine order, it was necessary for Erma to submit herself to me, her husband, as head of the home. However, in order for that submission to be valid, I needed to find my place in the Body. And with our varied ministry, constantly shifting and changing with no one local church to which we felt we owed any allegiance, where was my cover?

Should I really make a complete break with the Episcopal church, as I had been so tempted to do, and join some other fellowship? I felt drawn to the Resurrection Lutheran Church in Charlotte where the gifts of the Spirit flowed so beautifully. I was also attracted to the newly organized Trinity Assembly of God Church which was gathering in a little new building to worship God in the fullness of the Spirit. St. Giles Presbyterian Church in Charlotte was blossoming into life in a similar move of God's Spirit, and I had even been tempted to move to Naples, Florida, or Kingston, New York, to join with a free group of believers who without denominational affiliation were establishing New Testament principles in a local body ministry. Where was my place in the Body of Christ? It was a deep question, one which Erma and I knew must be settled in order for us to have our home in proper order.

One morning Erma woke unusually early. She had experienced a vivid dream, and her first question was, "Sherry, is there such a verse in the Bible as I Corinthians 12:18? I kept hearing it repeated in my dream."

I reached for my New Testament on the nightstand and quickly found the reference. "But now hath God set the members every one of them in the body, as it hath pleased him."

"It looks like God has already placed us, honey," I said. "All we have to do is find out where we are."

We knew God had been leading us gently and lovingly, but nonetheless firmly, into an ever closer and more demanding walk with Him. But there was still something missing, and at times we felt our ministry was just as shallow, ineffective, and phony as it had been in those early days of our marriage. We had been praying, "Lord, show us where You want us to be in submission."

I knew we needed the steadying, restraining, and sometimes pushing ministry which could come only as we were under the authority of a body of believers. Erma, to be sure, had me as her husband for her spiritual cover. ("But I would have you know that the head of every man is Christ; and the head of the woman is the man . . ." [I Cor. 11:3].) However, the very fact that I as a shepherd in the House of God had no cover myself, no one with whom I could be in a relationship of mutual submission whose authority I had to respect, made it much harder for her to continue to operate in an attitude of submission to me.

All through the years of our marriage, I had sought to find the right group, but somehow it had always eluded me. In the three years I had spent in Mexico just prior to coming to Charlotte, I had been under the headship of the gentle, undemanding Bishop Melchor Saucedo. But when I moved to Charlotte, I avoided close contact with the Episcopal church, fearful of being restrained as I had been restrained in Florida by my bishop. Thus I had not even made an effort to contact the bishop of North Carolina, nor to associate closely with any of the Episcopal parishes in the city. True, I had on occasion been invited to preach in Episcopal churches, and my new family had usually attended along with me. But it was obviously not the church of their choice, which made it all the easier for me to drift into the habit of selecting, week by week, the church to go to on that particular occasion—especially if the pastor or rector was preaching some message I was in agreement with. To put it plainly, we had become "church tramps."

Yet, for various reasons, I had never seriously faced the thought that I should leave the communion of the church in which I had spent my entire life. I was glad to be partaker of certain benefits—accrued to me as a retired rector, a priest in good standing (more or less) of the Episcopal church. And I depended on the church pension check I received each month for a large share of our living. However, I rationalized my position, actually glorying in being "above denominations," as far as my loyalties were concerned, and dignified this looseness with the thought that I was loyal just to Christ Himself.

Now I was becoming increasingly aware that there were certain positive benefits derived from belonging to a definite portion of the visible body of Christ on earth, even where that portion was far from perfect in its expression of the Master's full will. The more closely I observed the various portions of His Body, in the course of my ministering, the clearer it became to me that there was no such thing as a perfect church. All were made up of fallible human beings like myself. In all of them, some tares grew among the wheat.

The Resurrection Lutheran Church in Charlotte, even though it was a charismatic congregation moving deeply in the Spirit, was still bound to the Missouri Synod. St. Giles was very much a Presbyterian church, and for that matter, Trinity Assembly of God was equally denominational. Their backgrounds were simply not for me. Where, I began to wonder almost frantically, could I find *my* covering—and be comfortable in submitting to it?

In the summer of 1973, Erma and I attended the Tennessee-Georgia Christian Camp at Rock Eagle, Georgia. It was a great gathering from all denominations, with almost fifteen hundred people present. The closing service of the week was Holy Communion. The minister's sermon that morning was on the theme of finding one's rightful place in the visible portion of Christ's Body on earth. He dwelt on the importance of Spirit-filled Christians operating in submission to whatever local Body God had placed them in.

"Even if the pastor is not himself Spirit-filled and doesn't understand your Pentecostal experience," he said, "it is still better to yield in submission than to develop pride and rebellion by asserting one's self as higher than the Body of Christ."

Suddenly I saw two things clearly. First, that it was God Himself who had blocked all my efforts to find a spiritual authority which would exactly suit me. For this would have left my rebellious nature quite untouched. Second, it came to me that the Episcopal church was where God had found me, had given me salvation, had touched me with the Baptism in the Holy Spirit, and had even helped support me in my later years. He had kept me in it through several crises, almost against my will.

Then, with an intensity and clarity I can hardly describe, I heard God speaking in my heart. He was saying "My child, My poor struggling sheep, stop your struggling and find your place in My Body. Accept the place where I have already put you. Stop judging your church. Begin to love it." There it was again, the same word He had given Erma from I Corinthians 12:18—"God *hath* set the members every one of them in the body."

I gasped out, "Lord, what would You have me to do?"

"You must first go to your bishop in central New York and be restored into full spiritual fellowship," He said in the voice spoken only in my heart. "Step by step, I will show you what you are to do then."

I knew that technically I still belonged to the Diocese of Central New York, where I had been serving at the time I retired from active ministry in 1957. The present bishop was the Right Reverend Ned Cole, whom I had never met. God was whispering that very name in my inner ear, and I could almost hear Him say, "Go to him, for he is a true man of God."

Was the Lord of the universe also interested in Episcopal canon law? It almost seemed that way.

I nearly crushed Erma's hand as I whispered, "Honey, I know where my covering is to be! I must go to Bishop Cole in Syracuse the first chance I get and begin all over, a true priest in the Episcopal church."

I was crying. Perhaps a better word is weeping. Tears were running down my cheeks and lodging in my beard. I could not stop them. But I was not unhappy. They were really tears of joy, for God had heard my prayers and told me where my place in the Body was to be. Strange, for the place I had been seeking so hard to find was the place I had been all along.

As the communion service progressed, I sat quietly, running a spiritual inventory on myself. What a hardhearted and rebellious person I had been. I had despised the authority over me in the Episcopal church. I knew that from now on, I must obey God in detail in a way I never had before, no matter how repugnant to me the curtailment of my liberties. Yet now I wanted to obey Him through His designated earthly authorities. No more free-lance ministry, and no more self-chosen "cover." God might place others in such a position in the Body, but because of my rebellious, self-willed spirit, He was sending me back to my denomination.

When we went forward to the altar a few minutes later to

receive the sacrament, I was glad that a priest of my church, Father Blatchford, happened (in God's providence) to be the one who administered the bread and cup to my wife and me. Tears were still flowing from my eyes. Deep conviction of sin was in my heart. I didn't know it was possible to be so happy and so miserable at one and the same time. Confessed as sin, my rebellion was immediately under the blood of Jesus Christ and washed away. Now I had to start walking out God's mandate.

Up to that moment, I would have said I was only looking for a "cover" in order that my work for God might be more efficient, and that I might be spared some of the pitfalls I had so often fallen into in the past. Now I knew the whole thing went much deeper than that. I needed to be delivered and cleansed from sins that had undoubtedly vitiated much of my testimony. And I saw more and more clearly what some of those sins had been. Rebellion. Disobedience. Pride. Dishonesty. And many more.

I remembered how it all came about. Eleven years before, I had been interviewed by the newly appointed suffragan bishop in charge of the Western Florida area where I lived. At that first session with Bishop Hargrave, I was hurt and surprised by his antagonism to my charismatic experience. However, I fully intended to submit to his requirements, even though he forbade me to preach or teach in any gathering for the next three months.

Yet I had become so accustomed to being a free spirit, to speaking wherever I was asked, that I promptly forgot his order when asked to speak in a Pentecostal church in Tampa several days later. Three nights after that, I woke with the realization that I had directly disobeyed the bishop's orders. I was sick at heart, for I had every intention of obeying him. I resolved to call him up and admit my unwitting disobedience, asking if I might not begin my probation all over. However, I kept putting it off and gradually came into a position of deceit and subterfuge—justifying myself each time I preached by saying, "I'm obeying God rather than man." A spirit of rebellion and contempt for lawful authority had taken over.

When the bishop found out and called me on the carpet in great anger, I took the course of opposing him and trying to justify myself by arguments from the Scripture, writing letters of self-justification, practically defying him to put me out of the church. Bishop Hargrave wrote all the bishops of the Episcopal church, including my bishop in Syracuse. I learned if I did not submit to Bishop Hargrave, I would actually be deposed.

Grudgingly, reluctantly, I agreed to his stipulations. At his insistence, I gave up the prayer group in my home and promised not to teach or preach in the diocese in which I then resided. Bishop Hargrave, in turn, informed the other bishops that I had submitted to his authority and I might therefore be allowed, at the discretion of each bishop, to minister in their respective dioceses.

All this led to my moving to Mexico where I had several fruitful years of ministry in Guadalajara, under the gentle supervision of Melchor Saucedo. Inwardly, though, I nursed a resentment against my church and from what I now understood, realized I had been in a state of rebellion all along. This is not to justify any man—even a bishop—who quenches the Spirit. It is only to point out that I reacted, not in love, but in anger and rebellion. It would have been much better for me to have simply left the Episcopal church, and my coveted pension check, than to have remained, receiving my money, and disobeying the dictates of one of its bishops. Now, just as God sent Jacob back to the place where he made his first vows, God was sending me back to my Bethel—the Diocese of Central New York.

Erma and I returned to Charlotte, and I determined to seek an interview with Bishop Ned Cole at the first opportunity. On my desk lay the week's accumulation of mail, and right on top was a letter from the Diocese of Central New York. It was a sheet of suggested intercessions for the coming month, and exactly in the middle of the paper were the words, "September 23: Pray for the Reverend William T. Sherwood, retired priest of this diocese." What a confirmation of my new relation to my church!

I wrote Bishop Cole and thanked him for the prayers of the diocese and told him I was praying for them, too. Then I added I would like to have an interview with him at his first convenience. An exchange of correspondence followed in which I told him of my rebellion and my repentance. He most cordially invited me to come and see him in October, immediately after the General Convention.

Even though the meeting with the bishop was still a month away, I knew I was more completely in God's will than I had been before. I felt different inside. I was already a man under authority, for no matter what the bishop might require of me, I was determined to accept it, however difficult it might be. For the first time, I saw clearly that one of the reasons one must be under authority in this free life in the Spirit is to curb the constant pride and rebellion that so easily creeps in when we think we have received a special revelation. How easily freedom degenerates into license!

Bishop Ned Cole, handsome, vigorous, and strong, welcomed us into his study in Syracuse. "It is obvious to me that
you have a source of joy that communicates itself," he said.
"Please tell me about it. Tell me how you found it. Tell me
everything."

I could hardly believe my ears. I had come prepared for
him to chastise me, swear me to silence, put me in
ecclesiastical chains—and he was sitting eagerly in front of
us, begging us to tell him about our life in the Holy Spirit.

"You have found something this whole world needs," he
said with enthusiasm, glowing with approval as I related my
story. "I am so glad you came. Whenever you are near this
section of the country, please come back and share with me."

An hour and a quarter had passed, but before we left, he
asked us to pray with him. We clasped one another close and
frankly wept with an emotion which we did not try to
control. Erma said as we left the building, "I'll never forget
the tear running down the nose of that beautiful man up
there." Neither of us had ever felt the Presence of Jesus any
closer.

I was not left in doubt as to whether I had heard the Lord
aright. There came, one after another, invitations to speak
and minister in Episcopal churches around Charlotte. After
all those years as a retired, on-the-shelf priest, I was beginning
again in my ecclesiastical ministry.

It started with an urgent request to take the services in a
vacant parish in Monroe, North Carolina, for two weeks.
Then other invitations—all unsought by me. I was asked to
lead a retreat in a neighboring diocese. Then I met the newly
consecrated charismatic bishop coadjutor of that diocese, the
Right Reverend William Weinhauer, whose warm friendship
led to many happy contacts. Through him, I received strong

encouragement to submit to the Forward Movement Publications of our church a paper I had written several years before but had been unable to offer for publication because of my Florida bishop's stand against the charismatic move. To my amazement, the paper was eagerly accepted for publication, and I was asked for more.

In every church, I had the opportunity to preach the message of salvation through simple faith in Jesus, and the empowerment for service through the Baptism in the Holy Spirit. One invitation always led to another, and new friendships were formed that are, I cannot doubt, for all eternity. Oh, the goodness and the faithfulness of God to take my repentance at the age of eighty-four, and thrust me back into the green pastures of service in the very church in which He had found me long years before.

In Charlotte, I began meeting regularly with the bi-monthly Clericus, a gathering of all the Episcopal clergy of Charlotte and the surrounding towns. I had not met with them since my marriage, for I had imagined they felt hostile toward me, contemptuous of my charismatic convictions. Now I found these same men, whom I had written off as unspiritual stuffed-shirts, were wonderful men of God. I rejoiced in their cordial welcome. How sinfully judgmental I had been, and what opportunities for witness—as well as for good fellowship—I had thrown away in my pride.

Before long, I made an appointment with the bishop of the Diocese of North Carolina. Erma and I had a truly enjoyable hour with him when he visited Charlotte. A whole new life of ministering had opened up within my own church.

The closer I came to the *attitude* of submission, the easier it was for Erma to hold the same attitude toward me as her husband. We learned in experience what we had previously known only in theory, that submission is always an attitude and not simply an outward act of obedience—something you are, not just something you do. In the last analysis, I had obeyed Bishop Hargrave in Florida, but inwardly I had continued to fight him. I was like the little boy whose father commanded him to "Sit down." The boy complied, muttering, "I'm sitting down on the outside, but inside I'm still standing up." A letter of frank confession and apology to Bishop Hargrave brought a prompt and gracious reply. I felt an inward glow of Christlike love at the end of this long-drawn-out feud. Praise God!

Erma, too, found that genuine submission brought security, peace, and joy to our marriage that we had never known before. This, coupled with my deepening love for her and my relinquishment of all rights, submitting to the headship of Jesus Christ, turned our once tumultuous and impossible marriage into a union of joy, peace, and harmony.

To be sure, there was still tension in our lives, but it was good for us. It was not tension between us, as much as tension between the still-resistant Adamic nature in us and the call of God, which is ever upward and onward. He calls. He pulls. We stretch. We grow. And praise God, we press on and on to the prize of the high calling of God in Christ Jesus.

Praise His Holy Name forever. Luvaluia!

For a free copy of
LOGOS JOURNAL
send your name and address to
Logos Journal
Box 191
Plainfield, New Jersey 07060
and say, "one free Journal, please."